AUDI TT

THE COMPLETE STORY

JAMES RUPPERT

The Crowood Press

First published in 2003 by
The Crowood Press Ltd
Ramsbury, Marlborough
Wiltshire SN8 2HR

www.crowood.com

British Library Cataloguing-in-Publication Data
A catalogue record for this book is available from the British Library.

ISBN 1 86126 585 9

Dedication
This book is dedicated to Denny and Chrissie Ruppert who bought an Audi 100LS and
are directly responsible for this book.

Acknowledgements
It is hard to take all the credit for a book like this. There are many others who went out of
their way to help, and in particular the good people at Audi. At Audi UK Robin Davies
was particularly patient when I bothered him about all sorts of TT-related nonsense
throughout 2002. Martyn Pass and Kate Dixon also smoothed things for me and Beverley
Holloway made sure that real life TTs were put at my disposal. At the top Jon Zamett did
his bit too. At the Audi Tradition Department Ingolstadt press office Christina Fuchs kindly
sent me lots of old pictures. Judith Nitsch at Audi AG in Germany tolerated many stupid
questions. Bobbi Czarnik at Audi USA sent me crucial American pictures and press
information.

Carly Farrell at Octagon Motorsports arranged for me to go to Brands Hatch and
'enjoy' several hot laps with the racing driver Johnny Mowlem. He kindly talked me
through and demonstrated just how to drive a TT properly. Matthew Prigg at Warners
Music and Sarah Page at Maybeline Marketing helped with important TT-related images.
Malcolm Hobbs at QEK Global Solutions helped me to take the pictures of the TTs on an
airfield in Oxfordshire. Marcus Robinson at Fontain Motors (Audi specialists) in the United
Kingdom for his advice over the years about buying and running TTs. Paul Horrell kindly
turned out his files and lent me unique pictures and information on the TT concepts. Mark
Schneider at Abt was very helpful providing information about their successful motorsport
programme.

Thanks to the hundreds of Audi websites around the world; Audi Passion and Audi
World are two which had loads of useful information. Thank you to all those TT fans who
run their enthusiastic sites for everyone's benefit. Tap TT into a search engine and visit
them all.

Dee Ruppert as usual provided huge support and advice throughout, and for the first
time Olivia Ruppert was able to help to check the manuscript.

Typeset by Florence Production Ltd, Stoodleigh, Devon EX16 9PN

Printed and bound in Great Britain by The Bath Press
Reprographics by Black Cat Graphics, St. Philips, Bristol

Contents

Introduction

Once upon a time there was a pair of stunning concept cars which were presented to an amazed world at two international motor shows. A few years later you could actually buy them and we all lived happily after. Yet this is no fairy tale, this is the true story of the Audi TT.

If the quattro had given Audi engineering and motorsport credibility in the 1980s, then in the 1990s it has been the TT which made the company sexy. It is also the car that got Audi into big trouble. Not since the NSU Ro 80 rotary engines self-destructed in the 1960s and the 1970s had any part of the Volkswagen empire ever found itself in such hot water. There were serious handling issues that caused an international recall. Less significant cars would never have recovered from the bad press, but the Audi TT was different and that is why I love it.

My own love affair with Audi began in 1971 when my father arrived home in a new Audi 100LS which really caused the suburban curtains to twitch. Saloon cars then were mostly dull, sloppy and technically undemanding excuses for transportation. Understated, brilliantly built and rather exclusive, the Audi was a car that really turned heads. Furthermore, the awful Austin Maxi aside, it gave us all a glimpse into a front-wheel-drive future. Audi largely invented the compact executive car right there.

In the late 1990s the TT did much the same by offering something very different. Until the TT arrived, everyone had forgotten that sports cars should look striking, deliver instant thrills and generally be very sexy at all times. Not only did the TT not cost a fortune, thanks to some clever platform sharing, here was proof that you could have a concept car parked on your drive and not go bankrupt by commissioning your own one-off dream car. Concept cars were generally half-hearted, publicity-seeking motor show stunts to keep the designers from rebelling. If you were very lucky then one feature, such as a door handle, might just turn up in five years' time on a more ordinary model.

However, it was Audi's refusal to compromise that ultimately landed the TT in trouble. Although sales are now well into six figures, the truth is that the TT has not sold in the numbers in some markets that Audi had expected. But never mind, because the TT is not likely ever to disappear without trace, and so far the TT story has provided a fascinating ride.

Universally praised for the purity and boldness of the design, few cars become an icon during their production run. Few others cars are used so readily as backdrops to advertising campaigns or are credited with influencing the design of an entire generation of sports cars. The TT has had an impact that goes far beyond the motor industry, even boosting the sales of Jimi Hendrix CDs. It is no exaggeration to say that the TT has become a contemporary cultural symbol.

The truth is, that if you buy enough copies of this book I can then go and buy myself a TT. I could not think of a more deserving cause. So here is the strange, exhilarating and uplifting story of just how the TT made Audi sexy.

James Ruppert
Norfolk, 2003

1 Pre-TT: A Brief History of Audi

To own such a noble vehicle is to have one's good taste and culture in some way legitimized – in the same sense as an upper-class Englishman might regard membership of a select club as evidence of his character as a gentleman. To possess an Audi automobile, therefore, is to respect the laws of *noblesse oblige*.

extract from the 1924 Audi Owner's Handbook

There is no such thing as a brief history of Audi. Mergers, acquisitions and World Wars all conspired to make the story of the company that now makes the TT a complicated one. The easy way would be to suggest that the TT actually has nothing to do with heritage and everything to do with the cynical product planners at the Volkswagen group who ended with the Audi brand name and some time on their hands. All they did then was to rummage around the group parts bin, design an attention-seeking body and retrospectively claim that the TT was an inevitable consequence of its illustrious past.

If that is what you think, then this potted history will do. So, just in case you wondered, the four rings of the Audi badge symbolize the German automotive brands of Audi, Horch, DKW and Wanderer, which were later combined under the umbrella of Auto Union in 1932. Audi did not emerge as a marque in its own right again until 1965. Auto Union and NSU merged in 1969 and became part of the Volkswagen group. Audi AG was formed from Audi NSU Auto Union AG in 1985. There, that will do, but not really.

A roll-call of long dead automotive names will not bring any story about the TT to life. However, an examination of the history of Audi helps us to understand exactly how and why the TT was made and how Audi finally became an exciting brand name. Audi is not a pure breed by any means, but the diversity of its origins and the influences from so many companies have all led direct to the innovative, prestigious and exciting marque we all know today. I shall not trawl too doggedly through the last hundred years of motoring, but aim to pick out the significant events and, most importantly, the particular models which are an integral part of the TT's heritage.

Ring Cycle

In the beginning there was August Horch who was one of the early pioneers of motoring. Before setting up business on his own, he worked for Carl Benz in Mannheim for three years as head of automobile production. August Horch & Cie, was founded on 14 November 1899 in Cologne and built its first car in 1901. In 1904 the company relocated to Zwickau. However, in 1909 August Horch was forced out of the company he had founded and then set up a new enterprise, also in Zwickau, on 16 July 1909.

Unable to use the name Horch again, he translated it (hark or listen, in English) into Latin, hence Audi. The company commenced operations under the name Audi Automobilwerke GmbH, Zwickau, on 25 April

The four rings of Audi symbolize the coming together of Audi, DKW, Horch and Wanderer under the Auto Union brand, not forgetting that NSU arrived some time later. It is a complicated story, but crucial to an understanding of the TT.

1910 and he built a range of high-quality, four-cylinder models that excelled in motor sports, something that has been a feature throughout Audi's history. A post-war revamp by Audi's technical director Hermann Lange coincided with Horch's departure in 1920. The cars were of high quality, but expensive and complicated to build. In 1928 Audi Werke AG was acquired by J.S. Rasmussen, the head of the DKW empire, famous for its motorcycles. In essence

Audi was refocused to develop simpler and cheaper cars. Indeed, Rasmussen gave a brief to designers to build a small car powered by a DKW motorcycle engine, with swing axle suspension, front-wheel drive and a wooden body – to be developed in just six weeks. Amazingly, this was done and the car went on to sell over 250,000 units, making it Germany's most popular car at the time.

Going for the mass market was the right thing to do since demand for cars in Europe increased rapidly. It was in this environment that Auto Union AG was created. On 29 June 1932, Audi, Horch and DKW joined forces to create the Auto Union. An agreement was also reached with Wanderer for the takeover of its automobile division. Germany's second largest motor vehicle manufacturing group had been created. Auto Union expanded fourfold in size between 1932 and 1938. By 1938 Auto Union had 25 per cent of the German car market, and DKW had become the world's largest manufacturer of motorcycles. As now, Audi was part of group of established marques, and that could mean only one thing: that components were shared between the brands. So the next time that someone points out that there are bits of a Volkswagen Golf in a TT, refer them to the Auto Union era.

Indeed, bringing these companies together meant that there was much more strength and depth throughout the model ranges. By 1935 all technical development had been transferred to a new central design office and central experimental department in Chemnitz, where the Audi 920, DKW F9, Wanderer Types 23 and 24 and the Horch

930S were developed. There was even a crash-testing programme, which had been instigated to make the cars safer, with simulated front and side collisions and a lateral rollover test.

Ringmeisters

A crucial element of the Auto Union legend was its participation and domination in motor sport. Each of the marques which had come together under the Auto Union banner had previously enjoyed some degree of competition success. Audi had won the International Austrian Alpine Trials, a world rally championship of its day in 1912, 1913 and 1914. In the early years of motoring Horch had

The 1938 Auto Union Type D with a massive supercharged V12 engine, which powered this 485bhp racing car to numerous Grand Prix victories. The TT genes are definitely visible here.

The DKW F9 was another important ingredient in the TT gene pool. A new 28hp three-cylinder, two-stroke engine and an impressively aerodynamic shape were both delayed by World War 2. Afterwards two versions appeared, one in the west and one in east (badged as the Industrieverwaltung Fahrzeugbau IFA F9).

excelled on reliability runs, while DKW notched up more than a 1,000 victories on two wheels.

Not surprisingly Auto Union decided that the new brand needed to take on the world at the highest level. First shown to the public on 6 March 1934, the enormously powerful sixteen-cylinder Auto Union racer was the world's first successful mid-engined racing car design. When Hans Stuck took a brand new car around Berlin's Avus circuit he immediately shattered the world circuit speed record. During the next season Stuck won three

Grand Prix and all the significant hill climbing events. By 1937 the size of the engine had increased to over 6ltr and it produced 520hp. This was in a car which weighed only 750kg (1,650lb). A new 3ltr formula was enforced in 1938, and Auto Union produced the type D, a supercharged V12 that, by the end of 1939, was producing almost 500hp, almost as much as that of its predecessor with twice the capacity.

Apart from Stuck, other drivers of these fearsome machines included Luigi Fagioli, Tazio Nuvolari and the legendary Bernd Rosemeyer, who was killed attempting a speed record in January 1938.

The rounded, purposeful shape of the TT can be seen in all of the Auto Union racers. The big grille, the four rings and the streamlined shape: it is no wonder that TTs look so good finished in silver.

End of the Union

Audi as a company was still at the cutting edge, experimenting with aerodynamic designs and streamlined bodywork. Although Audi were early (1933) pioneers of front-wheel drive, the brand's new direction towards higher-powered, more enthusiast-oriented cars demanded more powerful engines than the Wanderer-based units could provide. There also had to be a switch back to rear-wheel drive, since there was a limit to the durability of the front-drive universal joints, which could not cope with larger engines. The resulting 1939 Audi 920, with a new 3.3ltr six-cylinder OHC engine showed the direction in which the marque was moving.

As for DKW, it concentrated on the lower end of the market where its small, light cars were responsible for about 80 per cent of Auto Union's volume, and had 19 per cent of the German car market in its own right. Two-stroke engines and innovative, lightweight body and frame construction characterized pre-war DKWs. However, the truly radical, wind-tunnel-tested DKW F9, scheduled for a 1940 launch, would have been a serious challenger to the Volkswagen 'People's Car'. If you want to see where the TTs curves come from look no further than this car.

ReUnion

Not many got to see the DKW F9 because of the war. Auto Union's involvement led direct to the company's being dissolved in 1945 and

The DKW 3=6 in two-seater cabriolet form was built by Karmann and the rump is reminiscent of the TT roadster, although the powerplant remained two-stroke.

the execution of the works managers. Some directors and executives did survive and made their way to Munich. The nearby town of Ingolstadt was the ideal location for a large parts store. Preparations were made to restart production and the Bavarian State Bank agreed to make a loan. On 3 September 1949, the 'new' Auto Union GmbH was established. The Auto Union had now been completely transplanted from East to West Germany, and, significantly, was the only automobile manufacturer to be successfully reborn in this way.

The first product of the new company, befitting the 'back to basics' nature of the postwar German economy, was the DKW F89 L delivery van, powered by a twin-cylinder, two-stroke engine and front-wheel drive. It was the first van with the now familiar forward control cab. The all-new Auto Union was substantially different from the old company. The up-market Horch and middle-market Wanderer were no more, and the distinctive Audi brand was in a deep slumber. The public face of Auto Union was effectively the friendly, mass-market DKW. The good news was that its first passenger car was effectively the slippery-shaped DKW F9. Blueprints had been smuggled in from East Germany and parts were re-created, and the first cars came off the line in July 1950. In the 1950s the F9 was succeeded by the three-cylinder F91 and F93/94, still with a two-stroke configuration.

Interestingly, DKW got involved in racing again. Following a series of wins by the DKW

The DKW Monza, proof that you can take fairly modest running gear and put a pretty body on the top of it.

The Auto Union 1000 SP coupé in 1957 and Roadster in 1961 proved that the group has always dared to be different, even if that meant copying the Ford Thunderbird. The bodies were manufactured by the coachbuilder Baur in Stuttgart.

3=6 in European touring-car racing, two racing drivers decided to develop a sporty body for this successful model. Günther Ahrens and A.W. Mantzel designed a record-breaking vehicle based on the 3=6, with a lightweight plastic body specially manufactured at Dannenhauer & Stauss. The 980cc engine was tuned to deliver over 50bhp for racing purposes, although some engineers eventually managed close to 100bhp. Several long-distance speed records were subsequently set at Monza in December 1956. A limited edition of about 230 of these models was made available and named the Monza. The Heidelberg DKW dealer Fritz Wenk had them built by the local engineering company Massholder and later at Schenk in Stuttgart. They used a 55bhp, 980cc engine which was

good for around 160km/hr (100mph), which was matched by its good handling characteristics. Some prototype, open-topped Spyder versions were also made, but never sold commercially.

The Auto Union nameplate made its return in 1957, with the launch of the Auto Union 1000, a further development of the F series DKW. Admired at the time for its graceful, shapely styling, the Auto Union 1000 also spawned an attractive coupé, the 1000 SP.

In 1958 Daimler-Benz obtained a controlling interest in the company. In 1959 the 741cc three-cylinder DKW Junior was launched and proved to be very popular. The Junior's successor, the 1963 F12, had truly up-to-date styling and front disc brakes (rare on a small car at this time). When the Auto Union

11

1000's replacement, the all-new DKW F102, also arrived in 1963, the group at last had a range of modern passenger cars, but with two-stroke engines. This did not sit comfortably with a company such as Daimler-Benz which wanted to concentrate on luxury cars and commercial vehicles. Auto Union had a for-sale sign in the window.

In 1962 Heinrich Nordhoff, chief executive of Volkswagen, agreed to a takeover. The Wolfsburg-based company realized that this would give it a much-needed increase in production capacity, as well as ownership of one of its more serious competitors. By the end of 1966 Volkswagen had acquired enough shares to make Auto Union a wholly-owned VW subsidiary. At least it knew how to sell cars that people actually wanted to buy, even though it had problems of its own with an ageing product line. So work went ahead on completing the F103 – an existing F102 with a new high-compression, four-stroke engine developed during the period of Daimler-Benz control. To help keep the production lines going in the short term, however, Volkswagen actually introduced the Beetle to Ingolstadt, where between 300 and 500 were assembled each day for over four years from May 1965. It was an effective means of maintaining full employment when the outdated Auto Union models were not selling. In September 1965 the first four-stroke car to emerge from Ingolstadt was ready for its public launch. That was celebration enough, but much more significantly it also bore the Audi badge. Audi was back.

Audi Reborn

The Audi model range developed rapidly, at first around the original four-stroke car, which became known as the Audi 72 (based on its engine power). Resurrecting the Audi name meant that there was a fresh start and some clear blue water between the smoking DKW two-strokes and the sophisticated Audis. Later versions of the new range were the 80, the Super 90 and the 60, and at the end of 1968 the 72 and the 80 were replaced by a new Audi 75.

Meanwhile, after lengthy and sometimes acrimonious discussion, Volkswagen completed the takeover of NSU AG at Neckarsulm; the establishment of the new company, Audi NSU Auto Union GmbH, was backdated to 1 January 1969. This brought an innovative company into the fold. It could trace its origins back to 1873, manufacturing knitting machines. Neckarsulmer Strickmaschinen-fabrik, to give the company its full title, diversified into bicycles in 1886. Motorcycle production began at NSU in 1901, and five years later the first motor car was built there. Automobile production was halted again in 1929, to allow the company to concentrate on building two-wheelers. It was almost thirty years later, in 1958, that the production of cars restarted in Neckarsulm. Most memorably the company bravely pioneered, along with Mazda, the Wankel engine concept that was to be the brand's ultimate downfall. Most importantly, NSU had the TT model name in its coffers which would be valuable decades later. NSU also had the design creativity that gave the Ro 80 wind-cheating aerodynamics and a timeless styling which would filter through to future Audi products. Is that why the TT looks so good and will continue to do so into the future?

The future was something that Audi could now look forward to. Ludwig Kraus, the technical director of Audi, had a clear picture of how he felt the next generation Audi saloon should look. However, new model development was exclusively a matter for the VW engineers. Therefore Kraus set about designing the new car in secret. The clay model of it was 'accidentally' discovered in the styling studio by the board chairman Rudolf Leiding. No one was sacked, because he was so

The NSU Ro 80, first seen at the 1967 Motor Show in Frankfurt, was a totally new and epoch-making design. With front-wheel drive and twin-rotor Wankel engine, no wonder it was crowned 'Car of the Year' in 1968. A great design let down by a smooth but unreliable engine, NSU set the design standard for Audi.

impressed by what he saw that he asked Wolfsburg for special permission to undertake 'body modifications', then suggested that the VW group board of management might care to inspect the result. They approved. The new Audi 100 was launched in 1968. Much of the clean styling though could still be credited to the influence of Mercedes-Benz when they owned the company. But for the purposes of this book the most significant model was the 100 Coupé S that was launched in 1969.

Stylish, quick and sporty it was the most attractive car in the Audi line-up and grabbed the attention in the same way that the TT does today. It was a car of its time and in the mould of contemporary GT cars. The Aston Martin DBS may have been faster and the Fiat Dino may have had a Ferrari engine, but neither looked any smarter nor more expensive than the Audi coupé. A total of 30,687 were sold, and in all the 100 range sold more than 800,000 up until 1976. It was a pivotal car for Audi.

Long-term, the objective was to gain some of the profitable executive and luxury sector of the market. Audi's USP (unique selling proposition) was going to be advanced technology. In January 1971 the first double-page advertisement appeared containing the slogan which has since been so closely associated

13

Elegant, well detailed and with real presence, the original Audi 100 coupé was all those things and more. The style is timeless and it still looks the GT part today.

with the four rings: *Vorsprung durch Technik*, which literally means 'the technological edge'. In Britain the phrase became memorably associated with holidaying Germans getting to Spain in record time and without breaking down and putting their towels on the sun loungers before the British could get their Rover 2000s off the cross-Channel ferry.

The 100 allowed the Audi brand to regain a personality of its own. No longer was it necessary to pad out the production lines at Ingolstadt with Volkswagen Beetles. Audi moved into the upper mid-size class, and why not follow up that successful coupé with another tilt at the sporting market?

The Audi 924

The situation may have looked fair for Audi as the 1970s arrived, but a recession was on the horizon and Volkswagen had an ancient model range with no replacement for the Beetle in sight. Money was therefore very tight. Ferdinand Piech, who ultimately went

on to lead Audi and the Volkswagen group, was a nephew of Dr 'Ferry' Porsche and working on the research and development for the sports car company and had a long-term contract with VW. Piech was a victim of cut-backs and cancelled projects, but he ultimately found a job at Audi, at first developing the five-cylinder engines and then the quattro. But Volkswagen continued with the EA425 scheduled as a replacement for Volkswagen's 914/4 sports car, which had sold well in the USA (115,600 were built), although Porsche's own six-cylinder version struggled, and just 3,107 were built.

Porsche went ahead with the commission, but as the fuel crisis deepened and with the Golf not yet launched to international acclaim, it looked less likely that Volkswagen would actually want two coupés in their corporate line-up. Yes, if someone wanted a VW coupé in 1974 he could buy himself a brand-new Scirocco, so an Audi coupé was looking less than likely. Although the EA425 design was signed off as a VW car in 1974, it was all change and in February it became a Porsche project. It already had a Porsche designation in 924, the 4 standing for four cylinders, everything else about it was largely VW Audi, as in the original brief. The powerplant was the 1,984cc LT28, as seen in Audi 100s, reworked by Porsche with fuel injection and a redesigned cylinder head to produce 125 instead of 95bhp. The gearbox was Audi and so were the brakes.

The 924 might not have the four rings somewhere on the bonnet, but at least Audi built it. The almost bankrupt VW had overcapacity and some factories were set for closure, but Audi's former NSU plant at Neckarsulm took on the job. The rest is history. Cynical motoring hacks and snobbish Porsche owners constantly criticized the 924 as being just an Audi, or even worse, just a VW. Their loss was the gain of 135,000 buyers who appreciated the neutral handling, reliability, practicality and performance of this entry-level Porsche. After all, Porsches started out as adapted VWs and now a member of the Porsche family was also engineering an all-new coupé that would not only give the relatives a fright, it would also utterly transform Audi's fortunes and image. The groundwork for the TT was now being laid.

quattro

It was 1977 and Dr Ferdinand Piech took the running gear from a VW Iltis military vehicle and adapted it to fit an Audi 80 body shell. Code-named A1 it became the legendary Ur-quattro, literally, original quattro. Using the standard coupé's B2 bodyshell, the original plan had been to build just the required 400 for motorsport homologation purposes. However, the sensation it caused at the 1980 Geneva Motor Show, where it was voted the car of the show, and customer demand meant that it went into production. Parallels between the TT prototype's debut and the quattro's are

obvious. Only one was a runner, but Audi has a habit of listening to its customers.

The quattro was a technological tour de force. Under the bonnet was a turbocharged version of the fuel-injected, 2,144cc, five-cylinder engine from the Audi 100. Power went up from 136 to 200bhp and produced an astounding 210lb ft of torque at 3,500rpm. That meant that the quattro reached 96km/hr (60mph) in just under 7sec and went on to an incredible 224km/hr (140mph) top speed. In the mid range the 80–112km/hr (50–70mph) overtaking zone took just 4sec. At the heart of the quattro was the four-wheel-drive system that meant power was transferred to the road surface at all times and in all conditions. There was a five-speed gearbox with a normal front differential, which allowed for a difference in the road speed between the front and the rear axle when cornering. But to give additional traction both the centre and the rear differentials could be locked by a console switch.

So the quattro handled brilliantly, and looked the part too. Flared wheel arches, sill extensions and larger spoilers which all sat on 6in-wide, 15in Ronal R8 alloy wheels contributed to an aggressive stance. The bold 'quadring' decals on the doors and sundry quattro logos also meant that there was no doubt that this Audi meant business. Aggressive and uncompromising styling with technical excellence was a combination we would see again in the TT.

What made the quattro truly legendary was the way it transformed the face of rallying. The quattro's first full season in the world rally championship in 1981 brought victories in the Scandinavian Rally, the San Remo Rally and the British RAC Rally. San Remo was notable as being the first time a women's team (Michele Mouton and Fabrizia Pons) had won a WRC event. In 1982 the quattro swept all before it to take the manufacturers' world title, with Michele Mouton runner-up in the drivers' championship. The following

Aggressive, high tech and uncompromising. Here was a totally new kind of performance car that proved itself on the road and in world rally championships.

year, Hannu Mikkola won the drivers' championship in his quattro, and Audi were runners-up in the manufacturers' category. The crowning year was 1984, with the new Audi driver Stig Blomqvist winning the drivers' title and Audi taking the manufacturers' championship. This was the year in which Walter Rohrl led an Audi 1-2-3 in the Monte Carlo Rally and Audi's pioneering work on the quattro driveline was acknowledged with the 'Motor Sport Car of the Year' trophy.

Undoubtedly the quattro was that good. Not only did it win prizes, more than any other Audi it changed the way the world

thought about the company. It seemed apparent that any new Audi coupé would only be better.

New Coupé, Old Coupé

It seemed appropriate that Audi as a company was growing up fast. The final integration occurred in 1985, when the title, Audi NSU Auto Union AG was transformed into Audi AG, with the head offices transferred from Neckarsulm to Ingolstadt. An additional DM943 million was allocated to new investment, earmarked mainly for production technology and the all-new, fully galvanized

Audi 80, which was launched in the autumn of 1986. It provided the basis for Audi's new sports car.

It was 1988 and an all-new Audi coupé made its debut, except that it was not entirely all new. Underneath the new, high-waisted body was the suspension of the outgoing 80/90 models. It floated and wavered, was a stranger to composure and only the quattro system, when fitted, saved it from further embarrassment. Not only that, but the five-cylinder engine in standard tune was not sufficiently fast nor refined enough. Matters improved over the years but not by enough. The S2 version with a handy 230bhp was meant to be a 1990s quattro Turbo, but although it had the twenty-valve engine, the hard edge of the original was missing. The unthinkable had happened and the Audi coupé had gone bland.

2 Dare to Be Different

. . . the vehicle in the viewfinder was undoubtedly a Porsche . . .

Audi chief designer Hartmut Warkuss
on the Spyder concept

Audi's coupés are usually products of their time, conventional, almost elegant, and not altogether surprising. However, when the company dared to be different something wonderful happened. The original tasteful and elegant 100-based example was the quint-essential 1960s–70s grand tourer. A bigger engine would have been preferable, but it had started to push the aspirational buttons in buyers who liked the idea of a sporty, quality car. The quattro Turbo was quite simply a road-legal rally car. Justified purely on the grounds of rally car qualification, Audi created a new breed of supercars. That breed is still with us today, although the badges on the cars are principally Far Eastern. The original and the best though was and still is the wonderful quattro Turbo.

Less wonderful was the soap-bar shaped late 1980s coupé. Here was proof if you needed it, that playing safe and subtle is not the way to win customers and influence a generation of car designers nor inspire enthusiasts. However, Audis have provided real inspiration for some of the world's most creative companies.

Karmann Get It

The German coachbuilders Karmann, who had a long association with Volkswagen building cabriolets and later coupes, linked up with ItalDesign in 1973. They asked the firm to build a four seat coupé for the Frankfurt Motor Show. The basis was an Audi 80 and the dimensions largely mirrored the saloon car. The Audi Karmann Asso di Picche, to give it its full title, could have been the first truly jaw-dropping Audi since the aerodynamic experiments of the 1930s and the astounding TT twenty-eight years later.

The idea was to make a fully functioning coupé that Karmann could put into limited production. It would have looked the 1970s supercar part with obvious straight edge design elements from ItalDesign's original Lotus Esprit. The side view was a riot of trapezia, with a delta-shaped C-pillar and a dramatically sloped windscreen. Apparently the designer of genius Giorgetto Giugiaro regarded the shape as a living space and, while giving as much elbow room as possible, still wanted to taper the shape to fit around the occupant's head and feet. Significantly the bumpers were built into the body, made of plastic and painted the same colour. They were integral to the car, not an add-on; this was a design innovation that would not become the norm until the 1990s and help the TT to look so coherent. Also, internally-bonded glass meant that aerodynamically the car would be uncluttered and efficient.

Giugiaro did not run out of inspiration when he moved on to the interior, a criticism that could never be levelled at the TT either.

Asso di Picche: the earliest signs that Audi was committed to design excellence, a sort of 1970s TT with rather more right angles.

In contrast to the shapes on the outside, inside it all became rather cylindrical. The main dashboard was a cylinder with many digital read-outs. In 1973 it was as striking, challenging and truly innovative as the TT is now. Although Giugiaro was pleased with the results, he repeatedly repackaged the layout as proposals for other car manufacturers with success.

The Asso di Picche did not simply end as an exhibit in the Karmann museum, many elements of the design found their way into the Lancia Delta, which was essentially a four-door Asso di Picche, launched in 1979. All this proved that an Audi could be different inside

and out and get away with it. As yet, a radical Audi had to make it to production.

Quartz's Time

In purely mechanical terms the radical Audi coupé the world was waiting for actually arrived in 1980 in the square-cut shape of the quattro Turbo. The pumped up body suited the car perfectly, leaving onlookers in no doubt that this car meant business. But, of course, there was always room for reinterpretation, which brings us to the Quartz.

The Swiss car magazine *Automobil Revue* celebrated its seventy-fifth anniversary in 1980 and Sergio Pininfarina decided to make a concept coupé birthday present. At the 1980 Geneva Motor Show he saw the new Audi quattro and thought that that would make an interesting base car. Audi was happy to help and provided a complete Ur-quattro in the summer of 1980.

Between the drawing board and the full-size model things changed and small 75mm (3in) lights were fitted which are reminiscent of Pininfarina's Alfa Romeo coupé and Spyder. The resulting car was 30cm (11.9in) shorter than a standard quattro, but still managed to seat four and their luggage. The body was tested in the wind tunnel and had a not overly impressive Cd (drag coefficient) of 0.45. By using carbon fibre and sandwich construction, the Quartz was 90kg (198lb)

lighter than the quattro, but just as driveable. Tested in 1986 by *Automobil Revue* they got a top speed of 217km/hr (136mph) and a 0 to 100km/hr (0 to 62mph) time of 7.1sec.

Much less exciting was the interior: all the usual quattro gauges not very adventurously rearranged and just an upright slab of plastic. Pininfarina obviously expended all its creativity on the exterior. Indeed, the individual who dreamt up the exhaust, based on the four rings, deserves a special mention. At the 1981 Geneva Motor Show it proved that an Audi coupé could look different.

Aztec Two-Seat

But if you really want something different, you go to ItalDesign for a real showstopper.

The Quartz was a rebodied Audi quattro and driveable too, with its high-tech, carbon-fibre construction and an exhaust based on Audi's four-ringed badge.

Again an Audi quattro Turbo was the basis, but this time Giugiaro really was thinking outside the conventional boxy bodywork of the Audi coupé.

In 1988 it presented the Aztec concept at the Turin Motor Show. The special thing about it was that the driver and the co-driver were seated separately, but they could communicate through radio headsets. The five-cylinder engine was mounted transversely as a mid engine in front of the rear axle, which was an intriguing and at the time highly innovative place to put the powerplant in a four-wheel-drive car.

To get in was interesting because first you had to tilt the canopy upwards and then open the door. The 'black' area in the doors was actually transparent. For full weather protection there were even bubble-tops that fitted over the screens and clipped into the boot. It was a surprisingly practical car too. Steve Cropley writing in the June 1988 edition of *Car* magazine said:

> I particularly liked the Aztec's screens . . . For one thing, the surroundings are symmetrical, which pleases the eye. I could still communicate with the person in the next cockpit . . . But best of all was the complete lack of wind noise and near absence of buffeting at speeds up to 80mph [128km/hr] (as much as seemed reasonable to an Italian test driver in town . . . we could have cruised at 100mph [160km/hr] for a day's journey without any fatigue . . . Not a thing to try in your MGB.

The Aztec had such an impact on the streets of Turin as the magazine tested the car that an old Volvo and Fiat came to blows distracted by the sight. No wonder ItalDesign actually made some Aztecs. Around fifty were built and there were also two other concept cars based on the Aztec. One was the Aspid, a coupé with rigid roof and the Asgard, a van with eight seats, both with quattro running

Is this different enough for you? ItalDesign went out on a limb and created an Audi Quattro-based vehicle, which was actually built commercially.

gear. The asking price was a steep $225,000 or so.

Obviously there was a market for practical, yet eye-catching, four-wheel-drive coupés and roadsters. The TT was just a decade away.

Groundwork

In the 1990s Audi was still changing with the aim of gaining more independence from Volkswagen in marketing, sales and dealer relations. In 1994 the familiar oval Audi logo gave way to the much more famous four rings. Audi was becoming a global company: worldwide sourcing of components and services, design centres in Spain and California and the opening of an engine plant in Hungary were just a few of the projects undertaken to ensure Audi's long-term competitiveness. Another interesting development was the manufacture of the Audi 100 in China.

New markets were opened up in Asia-Pacific, eastern Europe and South America. The year 1991 was a watershed one for the company. Not only was it a record year for both production (with 451,265 cars built) and turnover (DM14.8 billion), but almost the entire product range was replaced by new models. The following year saw an even greater output – 492,085 cars. However, there was a blip in 1993 when sales dipped. But Audi was revamping its range and still at the cutting edge when it perfected a construction method that would enable a mass-produced car to be fabricated entirely from aluminium. That car, the A8, celebrated its world premiere at the 1994 Geneva Motor Show, replacing the Audi V8. Apart from being the world's first mainstream aluminium car, the A8 started the renaming process for Audi's products, whereby the letter 'A' would stand for Audi and the numeral would designate the body-size category.

The second car to receive the new nomenclature was the A4 in November 1994, replacing the Audi 80. Introducing five valves per cylinder technology, the A4 became Audi's most successful model ever. With an expansive model line-up featuring four- and six-cylinder engines, together with turbocharging and quattro all-wheel drive, the A4 was the first Audi to challenge the sales volumes of its established luxury competitors. Not only did Audi re-enter the compact luxury class in 1996 with the A3, but a new direction was still emerging. With increasingly severe market competition, Audi's existing brand values, while strong and compelling, would no longer be enough. The new dimension would be emotion – the building of an image outside normal rational influences, an image based on a unique combination of style integrity, design progression, technological innovation and superb quality. The result would be the opinion-leading and sometimes dividing TT, in 1998. This was the car that would change Audi forever. So where did it come from?

Porsche Baiter

The first indications that Audi could do something different – and, indeed, something for itself rather than wait for an independent design house to rework a quattro chassis – occurred in 1991. At the Frankfurt Motor Show it was not just the Audi Cabriolet, new Audi 80, the high-performance S4 nor the new 100 Avant that stopped visitors in their tracks. The attention was directed to the Audi quattro Spyder, not least because the company had hired the then Miss World to unveil it.

Painted in Jaffa metallic, it was designed by Erwin Himmel, who also had the Audi 100 to his credit. It seemed to have much potential, and at the time Audi said that it would build it if the demand were there; it was. It was also reported that the Porsche family urged the Audi boss and their family member, Ferdinand Piech to drop the two-seater. He allegedly argued back that the Spyder would be priced below the cheapest Porsche, something that came to pass when the TT roadster undercut the Boxster.

It was reported at the time that the annual production was to be somewhere between Lamborghini's 500 (a company which Audi now runs) and Ferrari's 3,000 cars. It was suggested that Audi would choose the Tatra production line in Czechoslovakia, where there was a surplus of skilled panel beaters and craftsmen. The engineers at Ingolstadt had originally conceived a mid-engined rally car before turning to the alloy-bodied road car in 1989. The vehicle displayed was fitted with a 174bhp V6, but the research and development team also toyed with a V8 and V12 with rumours of a turbodiesel. The target price was £35,000, Audi dealers even took deposits, but just two prototypes were built. The recession obviously had something to do with that decision.

The Audi chief designer Hartmut Warkuss gave some interesting clues at the time as to just what the company wanted to do in the future:

At Audi we talk a different shape language than Ford, Honda or Cadillac. German design dates

The first Audi supercar which almost got built. Potential customers were not surprisingly writing deposit cheques in their local showrooms, but the early 1990s recession killed it. Now they build Lamborghinis.

back to the clarity of Bauhaus; that's why we prefer a direct, clear and rational approach which is not subject to fashion. What we do well are consequent geometries, clear-cut structures and strong proportions. Graphic simplicity is also one of our declared goals, but at the same time we do want to address emotion and to show some muscle . . . In the case of the Spyder design exercise, the vehicle in the viewfinder was undoubtedly a Porsche . . .

Avus Calling

After the excitement of the Frankfurt show there was more excitement at the Tokyo Motor Show a month later. The Avus quattro was a design study finished in polished aluminium with a twelve-cylinder, W-layout engine mounted in the middle. The engine was a dummy but the W12 was scheduled to be 6.0ltr, produce 509bhp, get to 96km/hr (60mph) in 3sec and reach a top speed of 340km/hr (211mph). Given that the Volkswagen group now owns the Bugatti and Lamborghini trademarks and VW have plans to build their own supercar, the Avus certainly pointed to the future direction of the company. Then the Audi boss and future VW supremo Ferdinand Piech strongly believed in brand building and image. Supercars grab the attention even if few people can actually afford them.

Like the TT and the Roadster, the Spyder and then the Avus were launched at consecutive international motor shows for maximum impact. The Avus provided the best guide to the future design direction for Audi, even though the TT had yet to be sketched.

For some time Audi had been cooperating with the Aluminium Company of America on the development of a lightweight, all-aluminium production car. The Avus remained a design study, but the aluminium factor resurfaced with the groundbreaking A8. According to Martin Smith who led the Avus design team, the car's appearance at Tokyo was to take European design to the country and emphasize Audi's heritage. Certainly the way that the aluminium is contoured over the wheels recalls the shapes of the silver racers that circled Berlin's Avus racetracks in the 1930s. Most remarkably, the low roofline and forward cabin position is reminiscent of the TT . . .

3 Getting Started

Surprisingly, the two prototypes have undergone precious few changes between the first clay model and the final production version. You don't mess with a good thing.

Peter Schreyer (chief designer
in charge of the TT project)

'It began in autumn 1994', recalled the chief project engineer Ulrich Hackenberg, talking

Early concept sketches showed that Freeman Thomas and his team wanted to keep the car low, hunched and tightly structured, but some of the edges look a little too sharp.

to *Car* magazine's European editor George Kacher in 1996. Kacher was lucky enough to get a sneak preview of the TT and the TTS, as the roadster was known then, in the Anzo Burrego desert in California. 'Design came up with a proposal for a compact roadster and the bigwigs were impressed. They gave us twelve months to prepare a running prototype. Before the end of the year they had also accepted a coupé spin off.'

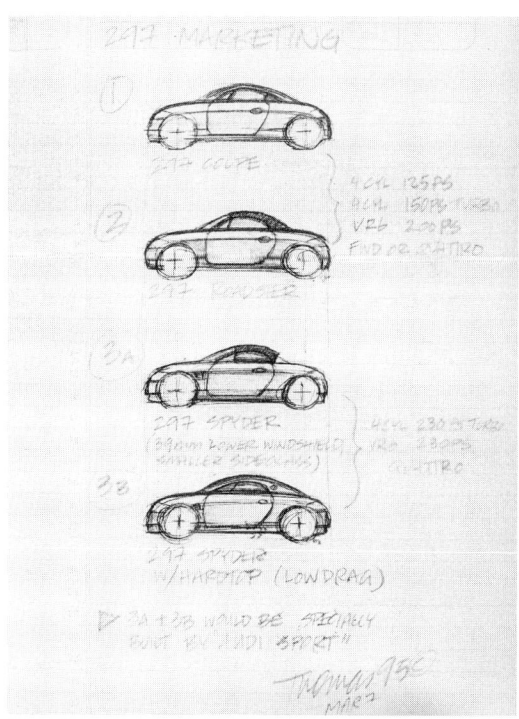

This is much more like the final TT as the lines get softer, but the TT is much more purposeful.

This begs an important question, namely how did design come up with that compact roadster to impress the bigwigs? The problem is that Audi press release publicity has not been forthcoming.:

> Note that the TT first took shape in the minds – or, better still, in the hearts – of Audi designers who have retained all their enthusiasm for an outstanding car, and who were given as much freedom as possible to translate their concept of the way Audi should build a sports car into reality.

Thomas Fluent in German

Audi wanted an image-enhancing sports car, but not at any price. The Avus was good, but would be far too exclusive and expensive, so it was left to the engineering department to come up with a solution. So Dr Ulrich Hackenberg and his colleague Ralf-Gerhard Willner presented the then technical director Dr Franz-Josef Paefgen with a proposal showing what could be done with a shortened A3 chassis. The designer Freeman Thomas was asked to sketch something over it and that was immediately recognizable as the TT. The roadster effectively sprang to life as a casual sketch, in the spring of 1994. Then, after intense, secret work in a German village called Gamersheim, it finally emerged as Thomas is often quoted as saying, in German, 'This car speaks German.'

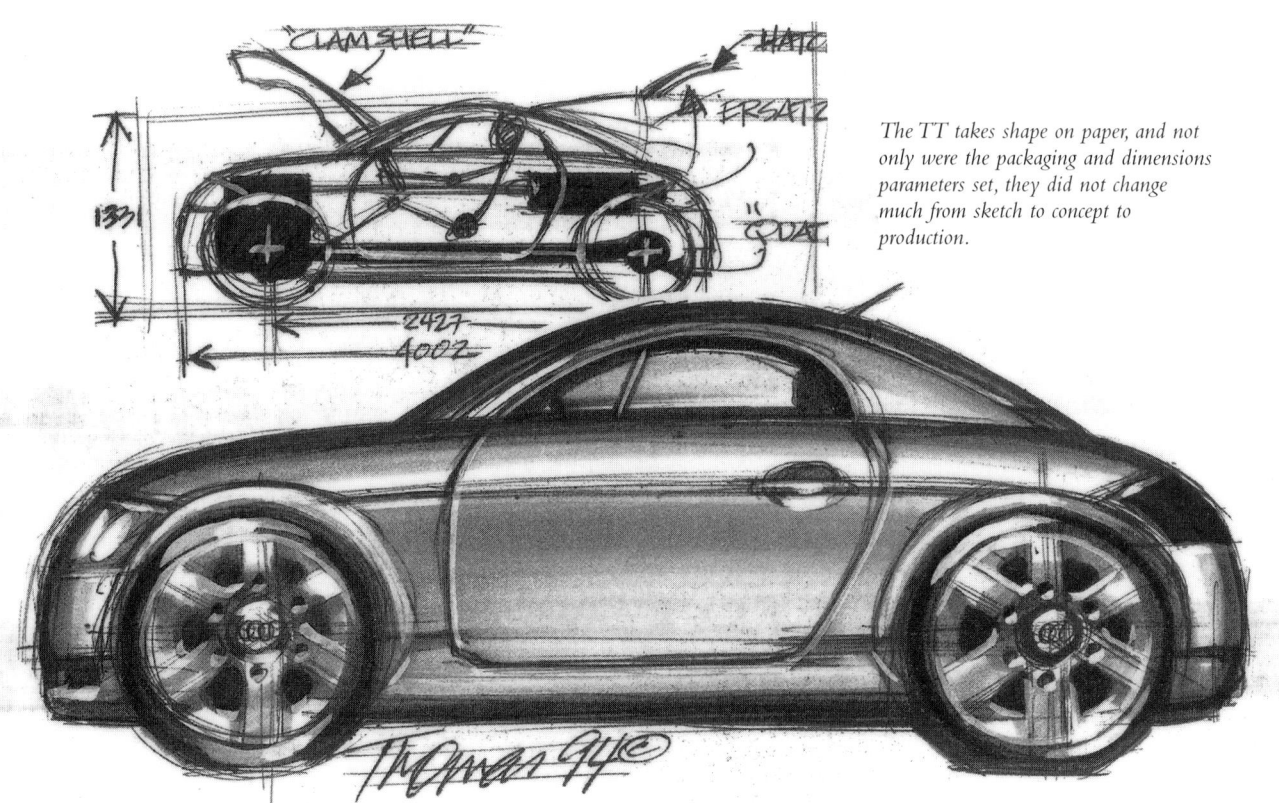

The TT takes shape on paper, and not only were the packaging and dimensions parameters set, they did not change much from sketch to concept to production.

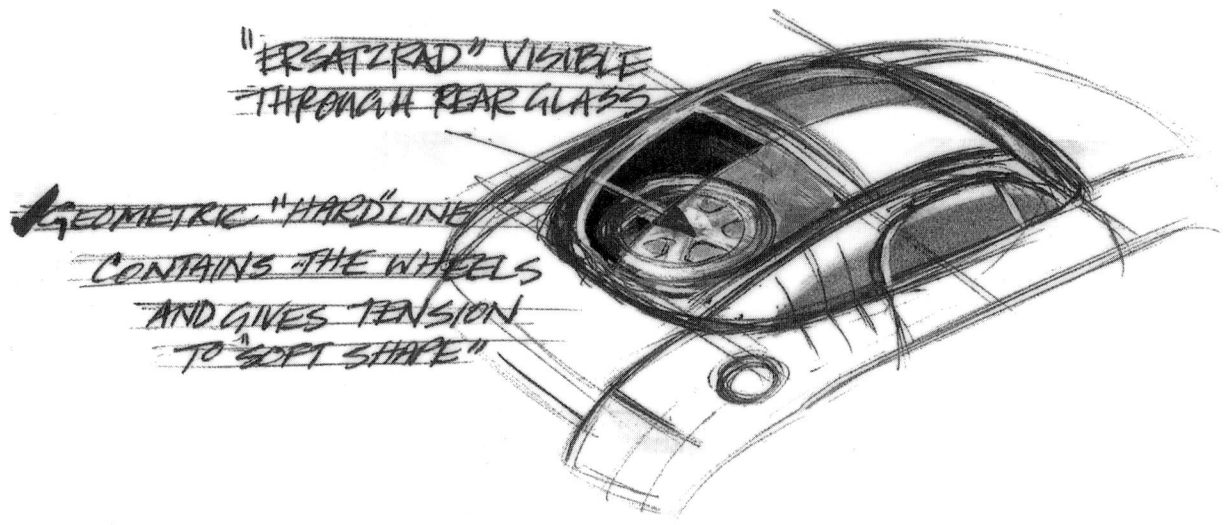

"ERSATZRAD" VISIBLE THROUGH REAR GLASS

GEOMETRIC "HARDLINE" CONTAINS THE WHEELS AND GIVES TENSION TO "SOFT SHAPE"

Not only did the TT emerge fully formed from paper to concept; many of the most important design details were being finalized too. In the case of the spare wheel mounted on show underneath the tailgate, it didn't even reach the concept stage.

The fuel filler cap, arguably the most distinctive single design detail, was being developed at the earliest stage. It was obvious on paper that it was going to work.

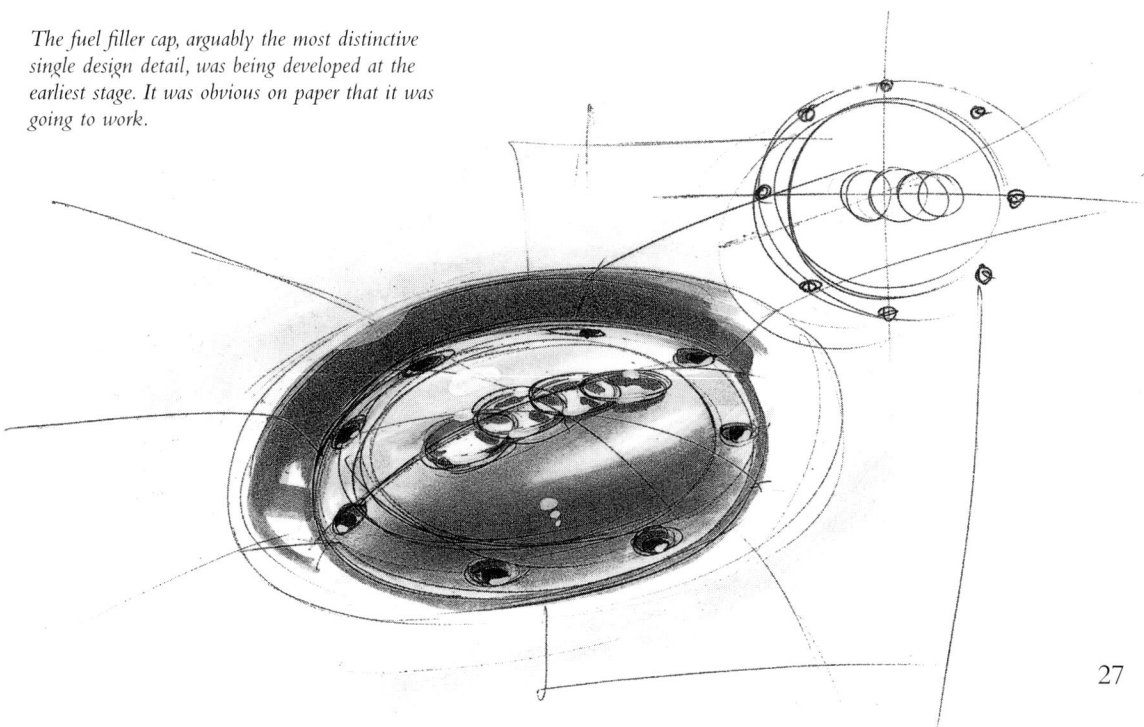

Thomas was in an excellent position to judge whether this car was fluent in German because he is the child of an American father – an air force air-traffic controller based in Europe – and a German mother. Thomas has lived and worked in both countries for long periods and understands the car cultures of both the United States and Germany. Because his father was stationed at several bases, he spent a lot of time on the road. At various times, the family owned a big Buick Roadmaster and a small Mercedes 190. 'Growing up,' Thomas says, 'I got a certain sense of automotive space.' It is no wonder that Thomas is credited with two of the most distinctive cars of the 1990s: the co-designer of Volkswagen's New Beetle, his other masterpiece is obviously the Audi TT. A *New York Times* critic called it 'historically significant' and nominated it for 'car of the century'. Thomas is exactly the sort of person you want as an automotive designer simply because he is obsessed by cars. His passion has always been for Porsche – also his first employer after leaving design school. It may also explain why some observers think that the Audi TT was originally designed as an entry-level Porsche. The simple fact is that the TT looks good enough to be a Porsche in that it is both purposeful and timeless.

Certainly the TT was designed to provoke a reaction. Thomas has said, 'It's what happened with the Audi TT: dismay . . . then it turns into religion.' Now Freeman Thomas is at DaimlerChrysler and his brief is effectively to stop American cars from being boring.

Two Concepts, One Goal

The Audi top brass had reasons to be pleased with what their designers had done. At the time the most attractive models in their range were a fairly dumpy coupé and an understated convertible based on the ancient Audi 80. Apparently they had considered replacing both cars with a range of middle- to large-sized models, in marketing speak that is the C/D sector, which would have squeezed them between the A6 and the A8. That idea went no further, so the engineers suggested coupé and cabriolet versions of the A4. That idea did not get any further either because Audi had already been down the conservative route with the existing 80-based cabriolet. Everyone realized that the TT and the TTS were just what the company needed. The decisive approval came from Volkswagen group head Ferdinand Piech who heartily approved of the concepts and the team that created them: Thomas (exterior), Romulus Rost (interior) and Ralf-Gerhard Willner (engineering).

So Audi had learnt the lesson of the Spyder and the Avus, which was: do not make a concept on a unique platform. If you do, it becomes prohibitively expensive to build. With the A3 earmarked as the basis Audi then made another important decision, which was to develop the convertible and coupé models side by side. That made sense, because subsequently to decide to launch a more profitable drop-top version of a successful coupé usually involves much expensive re-engineering. Not with the TT; Audi were getting two models almost for the price of one and neither was given preference over the other in the development process.

But first they had to make models. Thomas, Willner and two modellers moved into a small studio in a rented building not far from Ingolstadt. In two months the first quarter-scale models emerged and Piech gave his instant approval. There were no focus groups, no agonizing, just design purity. Thomas was instrumental in ensuring that the TT was distinctively German. That meant taking the Bauhaus route. Form and function were to be inseparable, although you could criticize the final design for being less than practical. This was not an uncompromising Bauhaus design, because these were sports cars and that meant

Strange things were going on inside the Audi design studio as they developed one of the most distinctive cars of the 1990s. Apparently Jimi Hendrix, or at least his music, was an integral part of the process as . . .

. . . they went to another planet . . .

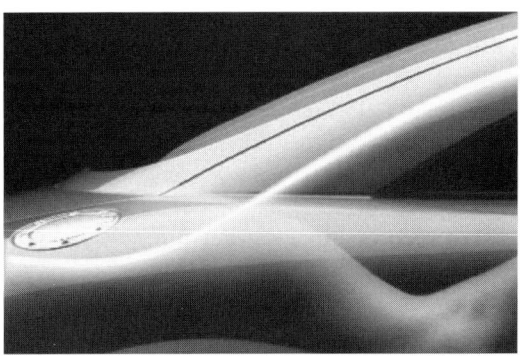

. . . and even used beautiful natural images to shape the TT (according to their TV advertisement campaign).

emotion and character were fed into the mix. At least there were no extravagant details nor even design cues for their own sake. Indeed, compare the TT with the rather too fussy Fiat coupé.

As the first sketches were revised, the final shape emerged in just eight weeks. We are told that Jimi Hendrix was part of the design process since his albums were played in the background. If he was in fact in any way responsible for the look of the TT, then his music should be compulsory in every design office. But not just Hendrix, but also Frank Zappa and Miles Davis, who also took their free-form turns on the CD player.

TT on the Inside

If the exterior was functional yet striking, then the interior had to match it for impact, or so one might expect. To complete the inter-national design team was Romulus Rost. Romanian by birth, he started work on the TT's interior in August and for the following month went to Audi's American design studio in Simi Valley. When he returned just before the end of 1994, his sketches, incorporating aluminium into the design, were greeted with some reservations. When interviewed about his work, he said,

> It confronts the onlooker systematically with a taut, compact dash panel. Its bold, arc-shaped instrument hood with its circular dials, in a layout that recalls the company's four-ring emblem, follows the curve of the steering wheel rim in a most logical way. The instruments themselves have exceptionally clear graphics, aimed at reduc-ing the visual effect to an honest minimum.

Aluminium was clearly the material of choice, already an integral part of the Audi A8. It almost defined the marque with its cool, stylish and understated qualities and was to be used on appropriate areas within the TT.

One of the last official sketches from 1994 which showed the final concept shape of the coupé.

The Audi chief executive Franz-Josef Paefgen apparently indicated at the end of 1994 that two side windows would be a good idea. It meant more light inside and a slightly less claustrophobic cabin, so the decision was taken to production-ready the extra windows even if the concept models never featured them.

TT Takes Shape

Thoughts were given as to the potential powerplants, and for the TT design study the 150bhp, 1.8ltr, four-cylinder, five valves per cylinder, turbocharged unit used in the A4 seemed the logical choice for what was to be a lightweight coupé. Indeed, weight was to be a major consideration and the design study for the TT. It had a load-bearing steel body structure with the attached panels, boot lid and bonnet all made of aluminium. They could have saved even more weight by omitting the rear seats, but it was decided to add a dash of practicality by offering back-seat accommodation. That consideration was never going to interfere with the clearly defined, two-seat roadster. Not only that, the designated power plant was a 210bhp version of the 1.8ltr engine.

In the early part of 1995 full-scale models were completed of the interior and the exterior in clay. A mould was made from them, the roof removed and now we had what would be called for a time the TTS. Once both concepts had been inspected and approved by the management at Audi it was time for ItalDesign to work its magic in Moncalieri, near Turin. It completed the cars in just four months, finishing in the last week of August.

ItalDesign is the legendary designer

The green-lighted roadster, with the distinctive front wing engine air outlets, which were regarded as a crucial part of the design at the time.

above and right *Cue the weird publicity photographs as Audi put the concept TT coupé into a power station. This was all meant to signify form and function: the power station looks the way it is because that is what it does. And here is a sports car that look just like a sports car!*

Giorgetto Giugiaro's company that has conceived some of the most important cars in recent decades. For the Audi Volkswagen group that included the Golf. Giugiaro had no design input when it came to the TT, his contract was to build the show cars and that level of confidentiality meant that even he never saw the TT until it was finished. Once Audi had given its permission, Giugiaro cast his expert eye over the design and pronounced that it was perfect. When Rost and Thomas asked whether there was anything that should be changed, he shook his head. Here was all the endorsement that the design team needed

that their concepts were going to have a huge impact.

Show Stoppers

The coupé made its debut at the 1995 Frankfurt Motor Show and has to be considered the star turn. Despite the appearance of the Lotus Elise and Porsche's new 911 Targa, all eyes were on the Audi stand. *Car* magazine described it in its show review as 'neat', although a picture caption also used the word 'brilliant'. It listed the specification, indicated that it was based on the future A3, but the

A different power-station view: rear three-quarter this time.

most telling comments were found in the last paragraph:

> The TT's young designers insist that every feature of the car is production feasible, another reason why we can almost certainly expect to see this car make production. When? In two years, once the decision is made. And the decision depends on

public and press reaction to it at the Frankfurt and Tokyo Shows. Let's hope we can count on it.

At that point the Audi management was mostly convinced that the TT should be given the green light, but it had another breathtaking trick up the corporate sleeve: the TTS. No one knew that seven weeks later it would stun

Together for the first and last time, the coupé and the TTS make a pretty pair, although there are changes still to be made.

visitors in Tokyo and only then would Audi be in a position to make the final decision. However, the TTS was not simply going to be the TT with its roof missing; the interior was going to grab even more attention.

In the earliest concept stages Rost had picked up suggestions that the baseball glove was a fascinating piece of design that could be incorporated into the design. Certainly form and function went together in the worn leather of a catcher's glove, held together with bold cross-stitching. It did not seem very Bauhaus, but when the rust-coloured seats were fitted to the dark grey roadster it looked perfect. Two steel rollover hoops and huge aluminium 18in spoked wheels meant that this car could never be overlooked. It meant that *Car* magazine could now write that:

> Audi looks increasingly likely to build the TT coupé it showed in Frankfurt in September, and

to emphasize the intent, unveiled a convertible in Tokyo called TTS . . . the TT and TTS could be on sale in '97. The TTs looks a bit like the two-year old Renault Argos. But that's no bad thing.

More to the point, the TT would actually be made, unlike BMW's offering at that show – the 4/2, designed by the Briton Robert Powell. With a framed aluminium chassis and extrusions and powered by a K series motor-cycle engine, it looked like a mad update of a Lotus 7. By comparison, the TTS looked pro-duction-ready. The most noticeable change was a triangular air outlet just in front of the doors. Rumours were beginning to circulate that Audi would build this car too, and it was suggested that the production name would be T2. It was no surprise then that the Audi board gave the go-ahead for series production in October 1995. Not that it was letting on. Ferdinand Piech, though, was quoted at the

Tokyo unveiling of both models that 'A few more years may elapse before you see both these design studies in the same place again.' Surely that meant that the TT really was coming.

Metalmorphosis

Fully operational prototypes arrived a year later when Peter Schreyer, the chief designer in charge of the TT project, explained to George Kacher just how the TT design had changed. Not only that, he also predicted how it would influence future Audi designs.

The TT and TTS are a good indication of the shape of things to come. They demonstrate Audi design is becoming more progressive and more emotional. I love these cars, even if I didn't design them myself. The shapes are the work of Freeman Thomas and Romulus Rost. I simply helped create the environment required to spark such convincing concepts. TT and TTS act as visual links between today's Audis – like the A4 and A8 – and tomorrow's models, like the next generation A6. Surprisingly, the two prototypes have undergone precious few changes between the first clay model and the final production version. You don't mess with a good thing.

The coupé doesn't need much more work. But we must still look at details like mirrors, bumpers and headlamps, and we may fiddle with the grille. The current solution is a little coarse; it may give way to a more detailed structure. But don't expect fundamental changes to the fixed head version. The roadster, on the other hand, is to undergo a number of detailed modifications. The provisional roof, for example, looked good at the motor show, but it would not provide protection in a thunderstorm. That's why we're working on a new, weather-tight, canvas top with a rear window. It must be easy to operate, light, cheap to build and made to match our quality standards. Unlike the BMW Z3, which sports a simple tonneau cover, I would prefer a tidy lid

that's both functional and aesthetically more pleasing. As far as a roll-over protection is concerned, we feel the tubular bars are a more honest approach than those active safety devices that pop up in case of an emergency, and which also cost a lot more money.

Although TT and TTS will use Audi A3 hardware wherever it makes sense, it is important to maintain a bespoke interior. That's why the dashboard is by and large unique to these cars. The invisible heating and ventilation elements will be shared with the A3, but the visible controls must be made to measure. The same policy applies to materials like the seat trim or the dashboard. In the course of the car's lifespan – five to six years, according to the product plan – we may make certain changes to enhance the appeal. These changes could be restricted to cosmetics like wheels, but could also spawn a high performance, wide-body version or a speedster with a different roof concept. Although no decision has been taken, it is clear both vehicles have a lot of potential. It's equally clear that the cars have already influenced other Audi projects. The redefined relation between body and glasshouse, the narrow (3.4mm) and geometric cut-lines, the long front overhang and the stubby rear ends are things you won't have seen for the last time. I'm really, really proud the cars have turned out so well.

Production Ready

Ulrich Hackenburg was the senior project engineer on the TT and the TTS. He took the show cars to the production line.

We started with a high percentage of carry-over items from the Audi A3, but since we wanted to offer as much room for the driver and front-seat passenger as the A4 there were many more adjustments necessary than planned. Take the engine bay, which gets its own visual treatment, then there were the A3 steering and brakes, which needed fine tuning, and the platform. For the TTS we beefed up the floorpan, shortened it,

opposite *The TTS as Audi revealed it to the world with unique door handles, mirrors, front quarter lights, the engine air outlet and a tiny hood.*

above *The TTS and the 'baseball-glove' leather seat-trim, which looked so inviting.*

left *Inside the concept TT and TTS was an equally jaw-dropping attention to design detail, superbly crafted and brilliantly executed. Often the interior is the first area of a concept to be changed for production as real-world costings start to bite. Luckily that never happened here.*

reinforced it again, and then adapted it to the front and rear suspension assemblies from the A3.

Normally engines don't need a lot of attention, but, when your goal is to find an extra 60bhp, you can't simply increase the boost pressure and hope for the best. You have to recalibrate the engine management, make sure the radiator can handle the extra load, install a larger intercooler. And if you touch the engine you have to check the clutch and transmission. In the case of the TTS, we also fitted a six-speeder. Then there's the 4wd system, which is VW's Syncro system, not quattro, so our boys had to start from scratch.

The integration of Steyr-Daimler-Puch hasn't stopped us applying simultaneous engineering to this project – the key to cutting development time from 27 to 24 months. Together with suppliers, we must also try to adopt the modular assembly concept conceived for the A3. Making the required changes takes huge flexibility but it can be done, although the TTS is further away than the coupé. For example, the production roadster will not get its own tyre size, brakes or front wings. Changes cost and at 10,000 units a year the budget is limited. It was hard enough convincing Audi that the hang on body panels should be made of light alloy. These things cost, but weight saving is a vital element of TT/TS strategy.

So Audi carefully took the concepts to production reality, but what did the buyer

The original NSU Prinz TT in full war paint and racing trim. It was also as successful as it looked, a real power to be reckoned with in European saloon car racing.

The new-generation TT – not exactly separated at birth from the original, but they certainly share a name and purpose as the Audi later made a big impact on the track.

actually get? Surely there would have to be some sort of compromise if the TT were going to work in the real world?

Why TT?

It is all about heritage. According to Audi, TT means *Tradition und Technik*. However, it is also a tribute to one of the legends of motor sport, the famous Tourist Trophy race on the Isle of Man and a direct link to Audi. Ever since 1911, NSU riders contested the motorcycle events, with frequent success. To commemorate this, a sports version of the popular NSU Prinz was named the TT in 1967. The TT was built at the Neckarsulm plant, which today manufactures the Audi A6 and the Audi A8. Developed from the standard TT model for competition use, the NSU TTS had a 1,000cc engine with a power output of up to 85bhp, and played a leading part in its class on the motor-sport scene. In 1967 it won the Tour d'Europe, at the time the world's longest rally. And Audi press material makes the connection clear between the old and the new products: 'Sporting in character, compact, a sprinter with a high top speed – all these characteristics link the TT models of yesterday and today.'

Audi TT and TTS: Concept Specifications

Engine

Configuration:	in-line, 4-cylinder, petrol engine, DOHC, with turbocharger
Displacement:	1.8ltr
Bore:	81mm
Stroke:	86.4mm
Maximum output:	110bhp (110kW); 210bhp (154kW) @ 5,700rpm
Maximum torque:	154lb ft (210Nm) @ 1,750–4,600rpm

Mixture preparation/ignition system:
Motronic, with sequential fuel injection and adaptive oxygen-sensor control; cylinder-selective knock control, mapped ignition characteristic; solid-state ignition distribution; 2 twin-spark coils; self-diagnosis system and emergency-run programme; fuel cut-off when coasting

Transmission

Layout:	transverse engine, permanent four-wheel drive
Clutch:	hydraulically-actuated, single dry plate, with asbestos-free lining
Gearbox:	five-speed, manual-shift gearbox, full synchromesh

Tyres:	7.5 J × 18/225/40 ZR 18

Performance

Top speed: (km/hr/mph)	TT: 225/139.8; TTS: 240/149.1
Acceleration: (0–100km/hr/ 0–62mph)	TT: 8.0; TTS: 6.0
Average fuel consumption: (ltr/100km; imperial gal/mile; US gal/mile)	TT 8.3/34.0; TTS: 9/31.4/26.1
Body:	load-bearing, fully galvanized bodyshell; aluminium lids and doors; impact-absorbing zones front and rear; additional side intrusion protection

Dimensions

Length:	4,002mm (157.6in)
Width:	1,751mm (68.9in)
Height:	1,345mm (53.0in)
Wheelbase:	2,428mm (95.6in)
Front track:	1,519mm (59.8in)
Rear track:	1,499mm (59.0in)

Kerb weight:	TT: 1,220kg (2,680lb); TTS: 1,240kg (2,730lb)

4   Concept to Reality

We always thought of it as a little grenade.
              Peter Schreyer (Audi Design Director)

Who would have thought it? That design study shown at the 1995 Frankfurt Motor Show which had such a rapturous reception for the sheer purity of the design actually made it to series production. Not only that, the concept car bore more than just a passing resemblance to the finished product in the showroom. To cap it all, the manufacturer responsible for it was, the Ur-quattro Turbo excepted, previously thought to be reassuringly conventional and supremely conservative; Audi had got the TT into the real world, almost intact.

Not surprisingly every component of the show car's skin has been subtly reshaped, mostly for engineering reasons. According to the Audi design director Peter Schreyer, interviewed at the launch, 'One thing would have killed it if it had changed – the sharp line between the canopy and the lower body.' That is because on most cars the rear pillar and wing are created from one steel panel. Schreyer and his team wanted to retain the sharp, horizontal, arc-shaped crease, including that acute angle at the back corner of the side window. They got around the problem by giving the TT a separate C-post and rear wing, which is joined at the crease by precision laser welding.

Indeed, the rear side glass is an addition over the original show car, replacing sheet metal. When asked whether this was to improve visibility, Schreyer replied, 'The second window was already an option when we did the show car. The long window adds Audi character – like the Spyder and Avus show cars.' So let us take a closer look at the kind of TT that finally made it to the showroom.

TT Power

When the TT was first shown at Frankfurt it had a 150bhp 1.8ltr engine, but it was always going to have so much more, hence Schreyer's comment that 'We always thought of it as a little grenade.' They took the Volkswagen group's turbocharged 1.8ltr engine with five valves per cylinder and set about developing it. This engine had always been blessed with an abundant amount of torque anyway, but reworking the unit was going to be fundamental to the TT's being taken seriously as a sports car. The major components were either modified or completely redesigned from the turbocharger itself and the intake manifold through to the electronic engine-management-control unit. The result has been a power improvement to 180bhp and, in its more powerful guise, to no less than 225bhp. So how did they achieve this?

AVL Powertrain Engineering can take some of the credit. Austria-based AVL is the world's largest independent company developing powertrain systems. Its contribution was acknowledged by Audi AG for outstanding efforts in supporting the development of

No introduction needed, here was the TT as it was pictured for the British launch. The changes seemed minimal to the metalwork, with the addition of the rear windows as the most obvious. However, underneath the body was some thoroughly reworked running gear.

the engine for the acclaimed 225bhp version of the 1.8 engine. The presentation of the Audi Quality Awards for 1999 was made during the dealer launch of the 2001 Audi A4 models in Lisbon. The citation for the award to AVL, presented by the Audi chief executive Franz-Josef Paefgen, mentioned the long relationship which has existed between the companies and specifically praised the system development competence shown by AVL. It also highlighted the smooth cooperation between AVL and Audi's engine development engineers during the project, from concept through to final production release of the unit.

'Although often bound by strict client confidentiality requirements, AVL is pleased to have been acknowledged for its contribution to the creation of the remarkable 225bhp 1.8ltr engine for the Audi TT coupé and Roadster', explained Frank Mundorff, AVL vice president of passenger car powertrains, 'AVL is very proud to be given this honour. As a result of this award, we look forward to the challenge of further collaboration projects with Audi in the future.' Indeed, those confidentiality agreements are binding and AVL declined to go into any detail about what they had done with Audi. The clues are, as they say, out there.

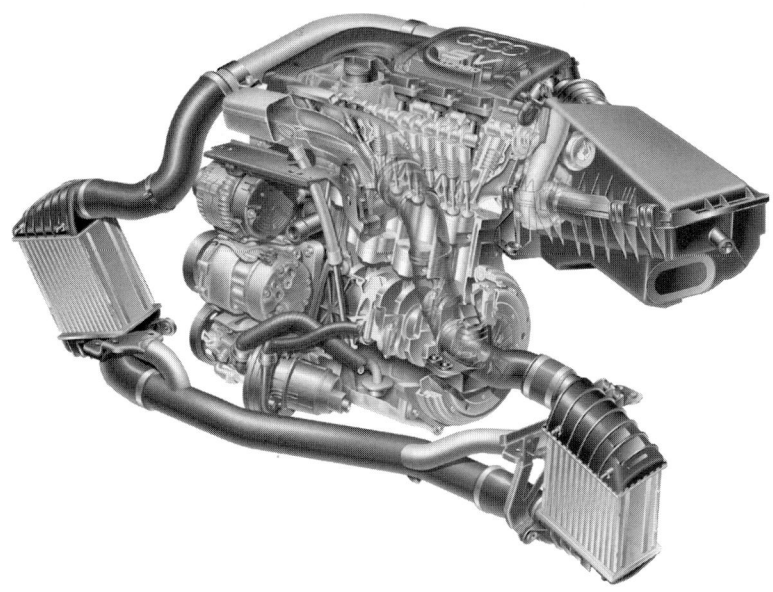

This is what the 225bhp unit really looks like. A look under the bonnet is not very rewarding because it is hidden away beneath black designer covers. Here you can clearly see the larger air cleaners.

One of the most significant technical features, and something that Audi has always been noted for in their turbocharged engine design, are the revised inlet ports. They impart a so-called 'tumble effect' to the charge air as it enters the combustion chamber. This increases the speed of the combustion process and ensures more complete combustion. The engine's efficiency is increased, and not only that, its pollutant emissions are lowered.

These Audi turbocharged engines feature the latest generation of electronic engine-management, Motronic ME 7.5. This adaptive system controls many important functions: throttle butterfly position, boost pressure control, sequential fuel injection with air mass measurement by means of a hot-film sensor, mapped ignition characteristic with solid-state, high-tension distribution system, including individual coils for each cylinder, and cylinder-selective knock control with two sensors. Effectively the engine management system senses the amount of torque which the driver wishes to have transmitted to the driven wheels, and decides how this can be

effected rapidly yet economically. The system then adjusts the throttle butterfly position, turbocharger boost pressure and ignition timing to the most suitable settings.

TT 225

So there was a choice of two 1.8ltr, four-cylinder, inline, five-valve, turbocharged engines optimized for flexibility and maximum torque. The top of the range engine has a useful 225bhp and an unusually high compression ratio of 8.9:1. Not surprisingly, the pistons, connecting rods and big-end bearings have been uprated to accommodate the higher combustion pressures. The double-mass flywheel and the clutch have also been modified to match the changed performance characteristic. The intake manifold, turbocharger and exhaust manifold are of an entirely new design.

This engine is equipped with two charge-air intercoolers, through which the Type K04 turbocharger forces air into the combustion chambers. Indeed, the airflow path is quite

Delivering 100bhp/ltr, the 180 unit is still a driving force to be reckoned with.

different from that of the 180bhp version, and, together with a larger air cleaner, ensures that the temperature of the air reaching the engine is only about 30°C higher than the ambient temperature. According to the experts, this is equivalent to more than 80 per cent charge-air intercooler efficiency, and keeps the engine supplied with an optimum flow of oxygen-rich air. The maximum boost pressure at the intake manifold can reach 2bar.

The 225bhp version's pulling power is particularly impressive, with 206lb ft of torque available across a broad speed range all the way from 2,200 to 5,500rpm. It really is a case of press and go. It accelerates from 0 to 100km/hr (0–62.5mph) in 6.4sec and has a top speed in the region of 243km/hr (152mph). It is flexible, too, needing only 11.2sec to accelerate from 60 to 120km/hr (38–75mph) in fifth gear. Interestingly, this is not only a powerful

Conclusive proof that the view under the bonnet of a TT is not as inspiring as either the interior or the exterior. At least Audi keep it simple. In case you wondered, this is the 180bhp engine.

engine, but a fairly economical one too given its performance, with a total fuel consumption of 9.2ltr/100km according to the EU 93/116 test.

TT 180

While the 180 drivers are still getting a useful specific output of 100bhp/ltr, this engine owes its rapid throttle response to a compact KKK Type K03 turbocharger. As engineers will tell you, relatively small turbochargers have a lower mass moment of inertia and are much more responsive. Because boost pressure builds up with less delay, there is none of that troublesome and frustrating 'turbo lag'. Torque at the lower end of the engine speed range is also improved, this being due equally to optimum throttle-butterfly and boost-pressure settings. The turbocharger and the five-valves-per-cylinder principle work ideally together, since the potential of the turbocharger can be utilized to the fullest extent by the large total cross-sectional area of the valves in each cylinder. The peak torque of 173lb ft is available over a broad engine-speed range from 1,950 to 5,000rpm. This enables the 180 TT in fourth gear to accelerate from 60 to 120km/hr (38–75mph) in just 9.8sec. Whether in front-wheel-drive or quattro specification, it accelerates from 0 to 100km/hr (0–62.5mph) in 7.4sec and has a top speed of 228km/hr (143mph), front-wheel-drive version, or 226km/hr (141mph), quattro.

We can thank the high compression ratio of 9.5:1 for these results, which not only ensures high efficiency but also helps to keep the fuel consumption low. This is (according to the EU 93/116 standard) for the front-wheel-drive version only 8.0ltr/100km.

Noise Pollution

Both of the engines available in the TT coupé qualify as low-emission units which is essential in a regulated world that insists on minimal pollution. The 225bhp 1.8 TT has a secondary air pump attached to the engine which helps to ensure that current emission limits are complied with. Fresh air is taken direct from the air cleaner and pumped into the exhaust ports, where a post-combustion process occurs. The energy which this releases heats the catalytic converter, so that even shortly after the engine has been started a high level of emission control efficiency is reached.

What comes out of the 225bhp's twin pipes and the 180bhp's single is not just an emissions issue, it has to sound right too. Consequently Audi's development team undertook a multistage 'sound tuning' process to ensure that the TT's power is communicated to the listener in a convincing way. The result is an unmistakable sound, which has been described as similar to the powerful rumble of a V8 engine.

Fourth, Fifth and Sixth on the floor

How did all that power get transferred to the tarmac? The six-speed gearbox, when fitted, with its close ratios, certainly helps as it redistributes the power via the electronically-controlled, hydraulic clutch for the front and the rear axle. This oil-lubricated, controlled, multi-plate clutch with its own oil circulation and electronic control system lies at the heart of the all-wheel drive in the Audi TT.

In both the quattro and the front-wheel-drive 180bhp versions of the Audi TT Coupé, a five-speed gearbox is used. The 225bhp engine transmits its power through a six-speed gearbox as standard equipment. This model features a three-shaft gearbox. Fifth, sixth and reverse gears are transmitted by way of an additional, third shaft in this unit. This new gearbox occupies less space than a conventional two-shaft design, but is capable of

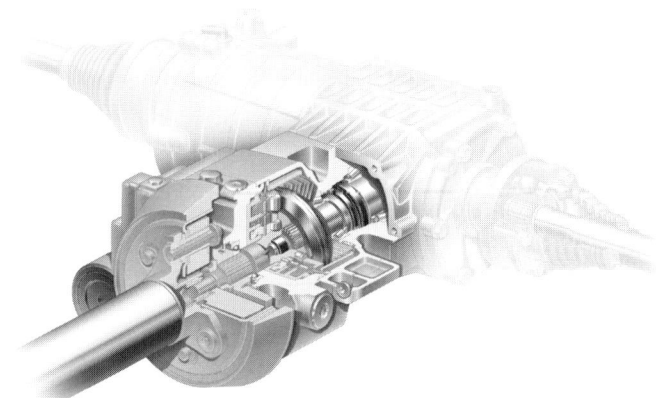

A cross-section of the multi-plate clutch. It looks complicated but it operates cleverly by delivering the torque to where it is needed, front or rear. Located between the propeller shaft and the rear-axle differential, an electric pump maintains oil pressure. So the higher the pressure the more torque is redirected to the rear axle.

transmitting high torques – up to 257lb ft. As a weight-saving measure, magnesium is used for the casing. Gears are selected by a wire-cable mechanism. This has the advantage that no rigid mechanical linkage is present between the gearbox and the gear lever, keeping vibrations to a minimum.

What Audi had clearly intended was a sports car, as even a casual glance at the dimensions and layout confirmed. There was the short wheelbase that is essential for maximum agility, the wide track, the large wheels with the wide rims and tyres, the low centre of gravity and the firm spring and shock absorber settings for a high level of dynamic stability. So all the running gear was tweaked in some important way. The front axle for the 180bhp front-wheel-drive car and for the two quattro versions is of the MacPherson strut pattern, with new forged lower control arms, new guide joints with larger-diameter journals, new cast steel pivot bearings and specially chosen axle geometry. Indeed, the anti-roll bar is pivoted directly on the spring strut at each side.

quattro in Name Only

Audi's familiar and well-proven quattro four-wheel-drive system was, as has been pointed out, not appropriate for the new sports car.

It was too large, too heavy and could not work with the TT's transverse engine layout. The exceptionally short body overhangs call for a transverse engine layout, but the real restriction was that the A3 floorpan was the basis of the TT. There was the option of Volkswagen's Syncro system, but it was dismissed because the handling was not appropriate for an overtly sports set-up. So Audi adopted a new system developed by the Swedish component maker Haldex.

Thus the TT coupé quattro incorporated for the first time an electro-hydraulically-controlled torque-distribution system. In theory, it has the same advantages and abilities as previous quattro models and is extremely compact. The ability to respond rapidly is achieved by exceptional sensitivity: so before the difference in the angles of rotation of the shafts connected to the front and the rear axle has changed by more than 45 degrees, the system is able to respond to sudden changes in road conditions. Therefore, if any slip occurs at the front wheels so that full traction is no longer available, the torque distribution system takes effect and redirects an increasing amount of engine torque to the rear axle in a precisely controlled process. By the time this change in torque distribution takes effect, the wheel has, in fact, rotated just 25cm (10in) further.

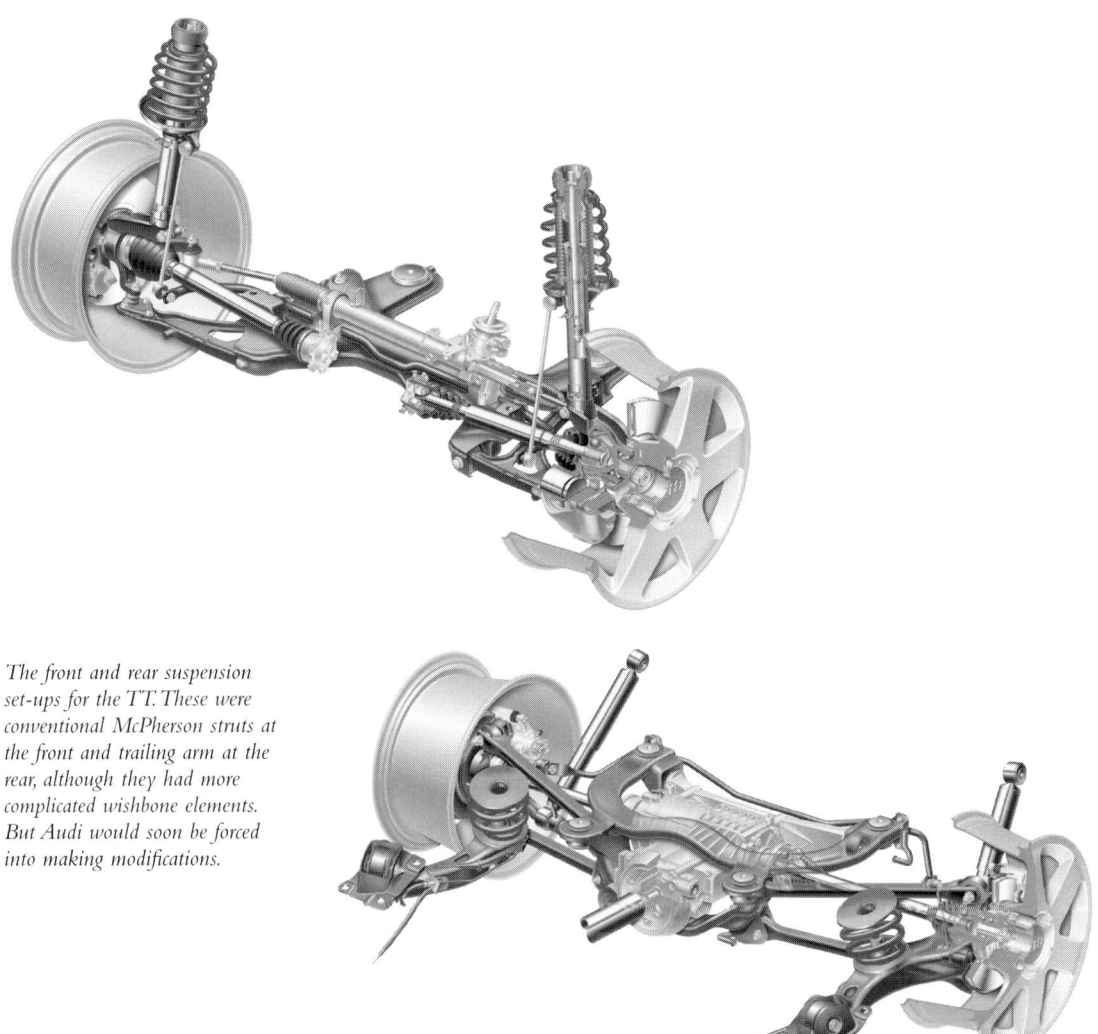

The front and rear suspension set-ups for the TT. These were conventional McPherson struts at the front and trailing arm at the rear, although they had more complicated wishbone elements. But Audi would soon be forced into making modifications.

The hydraulic multi-plate clutch is controlled electronically and installed between the prop-shaft and the rear-axle differential. Inside its housing is a plate cluster running in an oil bath. This can be forced together by a controlled increase in hydraulic pressure, so that it is capable of transmitting an increasing amount of torque to the rear axle. In addition, an electric pre-load pump maintains pressure, which ensures that the clutch responds rapidly. The greater the pressure applied, the greater the torque redistributed from the front to the rear axle. Essentially this is a dynamic system where torque levels are controlled by a variety of parameters. Two axial-piston pumps supply the pressure to the pistons, which operate the clutch plates. These pumps are driven by a swashplate which turns when a difference in rotating speed occurs between the unit's input and output shafts. An electronically-controlled valve is capable of varying this pressure continuously. The associated control unit makes use of information from several sources, including the wheel rotation speeds, engine speed and engine torque.

Not only that, a software program overrides the system sufficiently to take the driver's requirements into account. This means that, when the clutch is released as the anti-lock braking system (ABS) kicks in, no further redistribution of torque front to rear takes place. Consequently the ABS regulating system is able to operate without outside interference. Interestingly, the Haldex system remains active when the car is reversed, so that maximum traction is always available.

Revised Rear End

Audi realized that the Golf's half-independent torsion-beam rear suspension is ideal for a cheap and space-efficient hatchback. However, it would never achieve the levels of grip and handling that were essential in a sports car. Therefore they developed a new multi-link suspension unit and mounted it on a subframe before attaching it to the chassis. With the TT quattro the suspension layout had a combined trailing and double lateral control arms. This is still a space-saving design, with the springs and shock absorbers mounted separately, the latter at an angle. True-running and compact in design, the rear axle for front-wheel-drive cars has torsion-crank suspension. Track, camber and toe geometry were tuned to match the car's sporting character. Both rear-axle versions include an anti-roll bar which further increased the resistance to body roll, already bolstered by the firm suspension settings. On the TT quattro the anti-roll bar is pivoted to the wheel hub backplate by means of a

connecting linkage at each side, on front-wheel-drive cars a tubular anti-roll bar is welded into the rear axle assembly.

Helping the TT stick to the road are 205/55 R16 or 225/45 ZR 17 tyres, supplied with cast aluminium wheels (7J×16in or 7.5J×17in), styled exclusively for the Audi TT. Their spokes are attached at the outer edge of the rim, so that the wheels look even larger and emphasize the TT's sporting character.

Safe TT

Bringing the TT to a halt are disc brakes at front and rear. The front discs are ventilated and on the more powerful 225bhp and the quattro version the rears also had vital ventilation. Indeed, the brake disc diameters of 312mm (12.3in) at the front and 256mm (10.1in) at the rear take the car's high performance into account. The fist-type rear brake calipers are made of aluminium. This saves weight, in particular unsprung mass at the wheels, so that oscillation is reduced and dynamic stability improved. Heat dissipation is also better when the brakes are subject to severe loads.

Backing up the brakes were the electronic assistants that would ensure optimal traction, dynamic stability and safety, whatever the conditions. That is why all TTs had anti-lock braking (ABS) as standard and also an electronic differential lock (EDL) in the front axle and electronic-braking-pressure distribution (EBD). In addition, the 180bhp front-wheel-drive version has traction control (ASR). The safety package did not end with the braking system, there was also a comprehensive range of additional features.

The TT Coupé was designed to comply with existing and future European and American, frontal and side-on crash requirements. For example, the European frontal crash legislation calls for an impact at 56km/hr (35mph) against a deformable barrier, with 40 per cent overlap. In fact, the TT Coupé was tested at the higher speed of 64km/hr (40mph), in accordance with the European New Car Assessment Program (Euro NCAP) and the FMVSS (Federal Motor Vehicle Safety Standard) 208 in the USA.

Furthermore, the TT fulfilled not only the 96/27/EC side-impact crash requirements, but also the European frontal crash requirements and the stringent American head impact regulation FMVSS 201. Giving the bodyshell structure particular rigidity are high-strength aluminium side intrusion bars, door sills of substantial cross-sectional area and a side panel which all together form a strong composite assembly. A tubular reinforcement behind the door – referred to as the 'trumpet' because of its unusual shape – supports the side panel against the floor and largely prevents any intrusion by another vehicle if a so-called sideswipe collision takes place. Should the car roll over, roof frame elements of generous cross-section resist intrusion in a similarly effective way. But should a side impact occur there are plenty of active systems to help. First, the driver's and the front passenger's head-and-thorax airbags come into action. They protect occupants from the head down to the ribs. These airbags are installed in the front seat backs and therefore well positioned in relation to the seat occupant's body, regardless of the seat position or seat-back angle. Pyrotechnic-action tensioners at the front keep the seat belts taut against the wearer's body if a collision should occur. Additional belt force limiters prevent the load imposed by the seat belt from becoming too high, even in a severe frontal crash. The front seat belts are also tautened in a side-on collision if this is violent enough to trigger off the side airbags. These keep the occupants in closer contact with the seats, which tend to move towards the centre of the vehicle after an impact. This reduces the risk of rib injuries. Thus these safety elements look good and

have a key function, which is largely the rationale of the TT.

The rear seat is certainly a squeeze for adult passengers, but just about acceptable for children, provided that they do not suffer from claustrophobia. It is authorized for use as a Group 3 child's seat (ages from about 4 to 12) and according to the ECE-R 44 safety standard. Thus children of between 1.30 and 1.50m (4.3 and 4.9ft) in height may occupy it without a raised seat and be secured by the regular lap-and-diagonal seat belt. Not only that, ISOFIX child's seats can be installed on both the car's rear seats, because there is provision for the standardized mountings to be fitted. However, if you wanted a child to be at the front with you, the passenger's airbag can be deactivated by a switch in the glove box. This permits a rearward-facing child's seat to be installed on the front passenger's seat if required. A yellow tell-tale lamp on the centre console confirms that the airbag has been switched off.

That is how safe Audi thought the TT was at its launch, but controversy soon started about the car, as question marks on its handling were raised. Was it safe? (*See* chapter 7 to find out.) In the meantime, what else made the TT stand out in 1998?

Ideal Home

Before stating the obvious about the exterior, a look at what is inside confirms that Audi kept its nerve and did not hesitate when it came to creating a radical and exciting cockpit for both driver and passengers, avoiding all the usual sports car clichés. The TT's detail touches are inventive, surprising and a delight to use. It is also stylish, elegant yet functional. There is well-crafted aluminium and a winning combination of Alcantara and leather trim. The windscreen almost seems to curve down on either side of you like a Le Mans prototype racer. On either side are the tiny, curved side windows. You feel either invigorated or claustrophobic. Everywhere there are details that set the pulse racing. The metalwork follows the racer style filler cap, which is held to the body with Allen-head bolts. Everything inside is circular, with dimples reflecting bolt heads. The air vents have round, dimpled, aluminium bezels that regulate airflow. Simply open and close them by dialling their surrounding aluminium rings by 90 degrees. The door openers have the same finish, while the cup holders are a finely made pair of aluminium circlets. The red instruments look slightly like 1970s LED displays, and there is another light which illuminates the under-dash area while art deco numerals on classic analogue instruments reinforce the TT's 1930s heritage. The radius of the steering wheel is exactly the same as the binnacle over the dials so the two arcs line up perfectly.

Justifiably proud of its involvement is Magneti Marelli, who started the development of the instrument cluster in 1996. The cluster communicates through multiplexed CAN serial lines to the other control units fitted on the car. It also integrates several functions that have now become essential, like the anti-theft system with a 'cryptographic' code (immobilizer), the automatic system that calculates the oil replacement intervals and the diagnostic system with alarm and failure display on a dot matrix monitor. The instrument cluster is also able to display information regarding the navigation system. The CD changer has a separate compartment in the side panel behind the driver, the audio system's amplifier is beneath the rear seat, and the first-aid box is easily reached when needed in the side panel trim behind the passenger's seat. Underneath the dashboard flap is a good, standard sound system, although in many markets there were four audio systems specially matched to the TT's interior to choose from. The Audi Concert with Bose Sound System, for example, has a total of seven loudspeakers including a centre-fill unit in the dash panel, a 175W, four-channel amplifier and four equalizers.

Ergonomically the interior of the TT makes perfect sense. To adjust the heating level one simply presses the rotary knobs on the dash panel in slightly – they are marked with a ring of illuminated dots – until they pop out again. As the knob is turned to vary the heat output, the illuminated dots go on or off in sequence. This is a clear and distinctive optical signal. The control panel for the automatic air conditioning has the selected interior temperature displayed digitally. However, adjustment is by an analogue rotary and rocker switch which always springs back to its initial position. This enables the air conditioning to be operated with a single, easy, hand movement, and continues the TT-specific style already adopted for the seat heating controls.

There is an interesting flying-buttress arrangement of aluminium and leather linking the dash to the centre console. The aluminium braces do not merely look good; crucially they serve a real purpose, adding structural integrity. The finishing touches are the sports-inspired foot pedals, which are fabricated from perforated stainless steel with rubber inserts for more grip. The centre console is made of Lustran. It is injection-moulded by Peguform Bohemia in the Czech town of Liberec. Bayer's thermoplastic harmonizes with the functional aluminium parts to create a unit that retains its shape over a wide temperature range. The firm bond between the plastic and the aluminium facings of the radio and the ventilation nozzles, for example, is achieved by a simple clip system. Lustran can also be readily coloured in any of the interior colours – this was an Audi specification. Consequently, any damage to the decorative facing is not immediately evident.

The Alcantara upholstery creates a deliberate contrast with the cool, shimmering matt finish of the many functional elements made from aluminium: on the gear lever, ventilation outlets, steering wheel, glove box and radio trim panel. The leather-upholstered front buckets with Alcantara inserts help to keep driver and passenger in position when the TT's handling is tested to the limit. The seating position is low but comfortable, although the upper mounts for the front seat-belts are not adjustable and too low for the comfort of some drivers. The view over the bonnet is not exactly marvellous, which is no surprise when what you are sitting in resembles the world's most stylish bathtub. At the rear, the seats are (not surprisingly) cramped, just about acceptable for pre-school children, although to fit a child's seat is close to impossible. Adults might tolerate a short journey, provided that there was only one of them, sitting sideways.

The Audi TT may have some rear accommodation shortfalls, but that is hardly the issue in such a focused sports car. However, unlike many sports cars that are hardly user-friendly, in the real world the TT is still a thoroughly practical proposition. Take a look at the easy-access luggage compartment: a clever folding mechanism in the rear seat bench enables the rear backrest to be half split or completely folded down; the latter doubles the available luggage volume without restricting the function of the adjustable front seats. There is up to 540ltr (19.1cu ft) of luggage space available (quattro: up to 490ltr [17.3cu ft]). Additionally, the smooth sides of the luggage compartment, for instance, are not interrupted by any bulges or recesses. The big, curved rear lid opens to a wide angle and makes loading easy, although the lip is quite high.

The Body Beautiful

What everyone saw at the 1995 German Motor Show is largely what we got. Few compromises were allowed to water down the inspiration of the original design, probably because series-production requirements were incorporated from the beginning. There has been more pretentious nonsense written about the TT than just about any other car. Audi got in first though, and it is safe to say

Superb detailing makes a big difference. Excellent ergonomics mean that everything falls easily to hand. The dimple Allen key design motif looks just right.

Another angle on the best dashboard design for a generation. Under that TT-logoed lid of aluminium is the radio, clever and stylish.

Good looking and practical, the spilt folding rear seat gave this sports car a real edge as everyday transport, although the quattro running gear reduces the spaciousness somewhat.

The original TT as viewed from the rear without the spoiler. Strong, superbly detailed and built to the highest quality, the future looked bright for the new sports car.

that, because of the compact shape, clear outlines and bold styling it was the 1920s Bauhaus school that received the credit by reducing the outlines and forms to essentials.

Audi's designers put the wheel at the focal point of their creative work and produced a body with what designers sometimes call 'wheel emphasis'. Seen from the side, the TT Coupé clearly reveals how the body has been effectively stretched over the wheels. The strictly geometrical wheel arch cut-outs are boldly accented. The bold, curved surfaces at

the front and rear also derive quite clearly from the wheels, as do the roof and window lines and the crouching silhouette of the occupants' area. The result is a low-slung sports car 4.04m (13.2ft) long, 1.86m (6.1ft) wide and only 1.35m (4.4ft) high, with powerful proportions largely governed by the crouched stance when seen from the side, the exceptionally short body overhangs and the reduced glass areas.

That aluminium fuel filler cap is the eye-catching detail. It recalls the quick-release

53

filler caps used in motor sport. The exposed Allen screws, however, are genuinely used to secure the cap to the body – this too is evidence that some form follows function in this aspect of the design.

Now it may look sleek, but aerodynamically a drag coefficient of 0.35 is quite poor for a sports car and perhaps Audi was storing up trouble for itself (*see* chapter 7).

Strong Body

We have already mentioned that the original sketches featured an extremely wide rear roof pillar, whereas the production Coupé has triangular-shaped windows at this point. These not only improved the all-round visibility but actually created a more free-flowing roofline, so that the entire outline of the car now appears longer and more dynamic. A slight increase in length at the rear also adds to this impression. Other visible differences between the design study and final production included a radiator opening at the front, which now contains a grille; the air inlets under the bumper now look larger and the rear lights have been repositioned.

Everything from computer simulation to laser welding was used to achieve high body rigidity values. But additionally the weight had to be kept as low as possible. Aluminium has been used to reduce the weight of the Coupé in many areas. The bonnet, for instance, is made from the metal, so Audi's experience with the A8 was obviously crucial.

On the face of it then, the TT really was a no-compromise sports car both on the inside and the outside. But how did it fare in the real world? The proof is always in the driving.

Audi TT Coupé, quattro (180bhp) and quattro (225bhp) Specification

Body/chassis:	two-sided, fully galvanized steel construction, multi-step anti-corrosion protection, aluminium bonnet		sequential fuel injection, hot film air mass sensor, solid-state direct ignition with multiple coils, dual knock sensors with cylinder-selective knock control, electronic throttle operation, fully adaptive controls
Engine			
Type:	front-mounted, transverse, in-line 4-cylinder, 5 valves per cylinder, turbocharged, charged air intercooling	**Emission system:**	heated oxygen sensor, activated charcoal filter, 3-way catalytic converter
Displacement:	1.8ltr (1,781cc)		
Bore:	3.18in	**Performance**	
Stroke:	3.40in	**Horsepower (SAE net):**	180bhp @ 5,500 rpm/ 225bhp @ 5,900rpm
Compression ratio:	9.5:1/9.0:1	**Torque:**	173lb ft @ 1,950–4,700rpm/ 207lb ft @ 2,200–5,500rpm
Cylinder block:	cast iron		
Cylinder head:	aluminium alloy	**Acceleration (seconds):**	0–60mph: 7.6/7.7; quattro: 6.3
Valvetrain:	DOHC, belt-driven, hydraulic lifters	**Top speed:**	224/219/242km/hr (140/137/151mph)
Firing order:	1-3-4-2		
Fuel injection system:	ME 7.5 Motronic(r) with electronic, multi-point,	**Combined fuel consumption:**	25/23/23mpg

Transmission	
Type:	5-speed manual with synchronized reverse, dual mass flywheel and hydraulic clutch
Gear ratios:	1st: 3.300:1/3.818:1/3.417:1; 2nd: 1.944:1/2.105:1/2.105:1; 3rd: 1.308:1/1.345:1/1.429:1; 4th: 1.034:1/0.972:1/1.088:1; 5th: 0.838:1/0.970:1/1.097:1; 6th: /0.912:1; reverse: 3.938:1/4.630:1/4.107:1
Drivetrain:	front-wheel drive or quattro permanent all-wheel drive
Steering	
Type:	rack and pinion, variable power assist
Ratio:	15.6:1
Turns (lock-to-lock):	2.8
Turning circle (curb-to-curb):	10.4m (34.2ft)
Dimensions	
Wheelbase:	2,422/2,429mm (95.4/95.6in)
Track:	1525/1513–1525/1507mm (60.0/59.6–60.0/59.3in)
Length:	4,041mm (159.1in)
Width:	1,856mm (73.1in)
Height:	1,346mm (53.0in)
Weight:	1,325/1,455/1,485kg (2,928/3,216/3,282lb)
Weight distribution front–rear:	62/38–60/40–60/40
Luggage capacity:	391/306ltr quattro (13.8/10.8cu ft [quattro])
Suspension (uprated in 2000)	
Front:	McPherson struts (gas-charged) with 3-point lower control arms, directly coupled stabilizer, negative roll radius
Rear:	torsion-beam axle with trailing arms, stabilizer bar, separate coil spring and shock absorbers (gas-charged), toe-correcting axle bushings

Rear suspension, FWD:	torsion-beam rear axle with trailing arms, separate coil spring/shock absorbers (gas-charged), stabilizer bar and toe-correcting axle bushings (available on 180bhp models only)
Rear suspension quattro:	parallelogram, multi-link independent, coil spring/shock absorbers (gas-charged) and stabilizer bar, electronic stabilization program
Brakes	
Type:	dual diagonal circuits with anti-lock braking, vacuum power assist, asbestos-free linings, electronic rear brake pressure proportioning
Front:	12.3in (312mm)/12.3in (312mm) ventilated discs
Rear:	9.1in (232mm)/9.4in (239mm) solid discs/10in (256mm) ventilated discs
Wheels/tyres	
Wheels:	7J × 16-cast aluminium, 5-spoke design/7.5J × 17 6-spoke design
Tyres:	205/55 R16 / 225/45 R17, space-saving temporary spare
Capacities	
Engine oil:	4.5ltr (4.75 US quarts)
Fuel tank:	55ltr (14.5 US gal)

Standard features

Exterior
– power outside mirrors with defog feature
– heated windshield washer nozzles
– body-contoured, 3-way headlight assembly with ellipsoid low beam and fog lights, polycarbonate lenses
– 2 front fog lights
– high-pressure, retractable headlight washers
– side indicator lights in front fenders
– fixed rear spoiler (from 2000)

Interior
- 3-spoke, leather-wrapped, sport steering wheel with aluminium centre trim ring
- leather-wrapped gear/shift knob and handbrake lever
- manually-adjustable tilt-and-telescopic steering column
- interior lights in headliner with fade-in and fade-out feature, time delay, and automatic activation when key is withdrawn from ignition
- illuminated glove box, trunk/boot, lighter and ashtray
- fully-automatic climate control system with sun sensor, dust and pollen filter
- power windows with power retention, 'one touch up, one touch down' and pinch protection
- electronic cruise control with coast, resume and shut-off feature (dependent on market)
- electrically heated rear screen
- radio frequency, remote locking system with selective unlock, remote trunk/deck lid opening, panic function, interior lights, alarm system activation (control integrated in folding ignition key)
- power central locking system (doors, trunk, fuel door), with selective unlocking (enables unlocking of a single door or both doors), plus convenience open and close features for windows
- front sport seats with manual height adjustment
- Alcantara or Valcona leather seat upholstery, including door panel inserts
- aluminium trim on centre dashboard vents, shift lever knob and base, knee bolsters on centre console, door release handles, radio cover, glove box cover
- 50/50 split-fold rear seat
- 2 tie-down eyelets in rear cargo area
- 2 aluminium cup holders in centre console
- tool kit located in rear storage compartment of rear cargo area

Safety
- anti-lock brake system with electronic differential lock and electronic rear brake pressure regulation
- driver and front passenger front airbag supplemental restraints
- driver and front seat mounted chest and head side airbag supplemental restraints
- front 3-point safety belts with automatic pre-tensioning and force limiters
- central locking system with safety unlock feature (if airbag deploys)
- emergency warning triangle located in rear cargo area
- first-aid kit
- locking head restraints for front seats

Electronics/instrumentation
- illuminated backlit instrument cluster with automatic brightness control, including tachometer, electronic speedometer, digital clock with date, service interval indicator; fuel and coolant gauges
- driver information display with 5-function trip computer, including outside temperature and radio/telephone displays, active Auto Check system with speed warning device and pictogram display for open door and trunk
- anti-theft alarm system with blinking theft-deterrent light
- windshield wipers with 4-position adjustable intermittent interval rate

Audio
- 80W Audi Concert AM/FM stereo with CD, radio broadcast display system, Graduated Audio Level Adjustment (GALA) and CD changer operation capability
- pre-wiring for 6-disc CD changer
- radio antenna in rear window glass

Options
- global positioning Audi navigation system
- Motorola hands-free digital portable telephone
- pre-wiring for Motorola portable telephone
- unique 'nubbed' TT cloth upholstery with leather bolsters (no-cost option)
- 17in, 6-spoke cast alloy wheels with 225/45 performance tyres (for 180bhp models)
- 17in, 5-spoke forged alloy wheels with 225/45 tyres (225bhp)
- Bose 174W premium 7-speaker sound system with 6-disc CD changer
- heated front seats with individual temperature control
- xenon high-intensity discharge headlights with automatic self-levelling

5 Lifting the Lid

For car lovers looking for the most authentic form of motoring–open-top roadsters – Audi has the answer: the new Audi TT Roadster.

Press release marking the TT Roadster's North American debut at the Greater Los Angeles Auto Show

In case you had forgotten, the Coupé was part of a set. The other TT twin, although by no means an identical one, was the TTS. Here was a car exhibited in Tokyo which tipped the balance in favour of a full-scale production run. What appealed to them in Tokyo?

Tokyo Calling

From the technical point of view, Audi's commitment to using lightweight materials continued with the engine and boot lid, doors, even the handbrake and the highly accentuated air vent rings, all made from aluminium. The paint finish, a dense metallic grey, which said Audi, aimed for function rather than

Ready for takeoff, but in 1995 it was still called the TTS. Detailed changes were required before it could be truly ready for production.

The production TT as launched, with only minor, visual changes.

effect, whereas visual accents such as the screwed-in 'Mille Miglia' fuel filler cap add a note of elegance.

The only exaggerated sports car touches were the two exposed exhaust tailpipes and the air outlets from the engine compartment on the sides of the body. To suit the TTS Roadster in its role as a pure 'driving machine', the brakes and the wheels were enlarged: the latter are 18in in diameter and shod with wide, 225/40 ZR 18 tyres.

It was clear that the soft-top had been pulled well down, almost like a peaked cap, needing only a minimum of supporting hoops, and had no rear window. Behind the occupants' seats was a soft-top compartment, which could also be used as extra luggage space, and serves the additional purpose of stiffening the Roadster's body. At 1,240kg (2,700lb), inclusive of permanent four-wheel drive, the Roadster actually weighed little more than the Coupé. Those two distinctive angled roll bars had a front support between the seats to add rigidity to the body and floor pan structure.

So what details survived the transition from Motor Show star to real world production car?

From TTS to Roadster

The first casualty was the name. Out went TTS and in came Roadster. Audi went to some lengths to justify the name. Two seats and a soft top are the minimal qualification for roadsterdom, but add some saloon car luxuries and you have a Cabriolet, take away just about everything including the windscreen and you have a Spider. So the roadster is something in between; Roadster was intended to describe open, two-seater cars for use on the roads and not on the racetrack.

Roofless Hood

From the beginning, the designers had regarded a roof as quite important. Originally, roadsters made do with a simple tonneau cover or perhaps nothing at all. The late 1990s driver was not going to put up with that sort of discomfort and why should he? Being a TT, the hood had to look good; that challenge was easily met by the designers and their peaked-cap approach. No rear window may have looked attractive on the concept TTS, but there was going to be much customer

resistance, however good it looked. The tiny side windows give the impression that the interior must be extremely cramped, but the dome of the roof means that there is actually plenty of headroom, even for occupants well over 6ft in height.

So the TT's soft top now had a large, heated, rear window. Even more significantly, it could now be opened in a single-stage process. Only one hand is needed to release the firm fabric soft top with its flexible panels and lower it down behind the two seats. The manual procedure takes roughly 10sec and is best performed while one is outside the roadster. Some may find it a chore: twist a handle, lift the front, push the top back as far as possible, then get out and finish folding the top. Also, the top had no lining over bows. Many prefer the power-operated top, which manages the entire operation reliably in 15sec. To ensure the hood's easy operation, it is fitted with an ingenious anti-theft locking mechanism, which can only be released after a door has been unlocked. Not only that, but a tonneau cover made of multi-layer synthetic material could be quickly and easily attached to conceal the soft top when open, thus

Just in case you wondered how it worked, here is the aerodynamic explanation for the optional retractable glass windbreak.

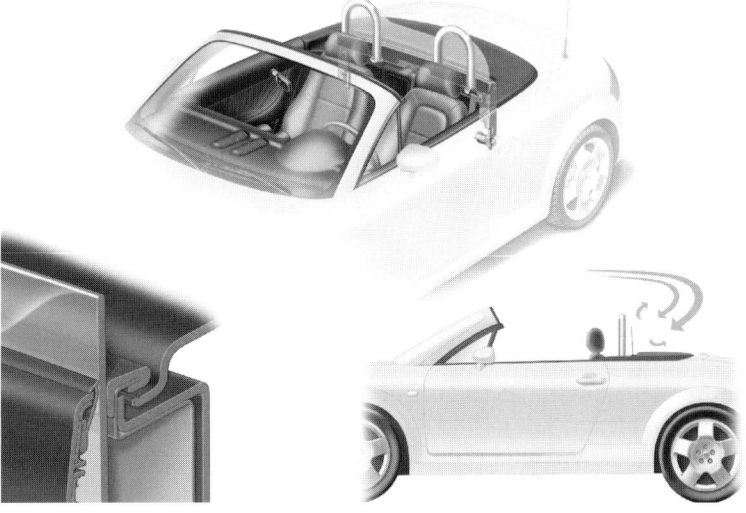

preventing the fabric and mechanism from getting dirty, and it can be stored in the boot when not in use. A hinged cover forming part of the bodywork would have been the obvious solution. But, according to the Audi designers, it would have necessitated a shut line, which was regarded as aesthetically unacceptable.

Turbulence, something that often disturbs roadster occupants at high speeds, was reduced by an optional, electrically-retractable glass windbreak. Something completely new, this does not break up the flowing lines of the TT Roadster. Unlike a net or gauze, it will not let even a wisp of air pass through it, but serves to calm turbulence, define the airflow through the cockpit and guarantee a pleasant internal 'climate' such as one would not expect to find in a roadster. The windbreak's profile perfectly matches the TT Roadster. With its two curves it follows the typical TT silhouette of the roll-over bars. And because it is slightly curved, it carries out its task almost invisibly and causes no stray reflections. The Roadster was now the most unruffled way to travel, at almost whatever speed the driver desired.

Roadster Power

Power was provided by the familiar 1.8ltr, turbocharged, four-cylinder, inline engines with either 180 or 225bhp. Acceleration from 0 to 96km/hr (0–60mph) in the 225bhp version was just 6.7sec. The front-wheel-drive Roadster can reach a top speed of 208km/hr (130mph). The 225bhp version, with its standard all-wheel drive, reaches a top speed of 230km/hr (143mph).

Just as impressive as the acceleration and top speeds of both models is their vigorous pulling power. The 225bhp TT's maximum torque of 207lb.ft. is developed between 2,200 and 5,500rpm and 173lb ft. of torque is available between 1,950 and 4,700rpm from the 180bhp engine. The well-chosen gear ratios ensure supreme progress, with a five-speed manual gearbox for the 180bhp front-wheel-drive Roadster and a six-speed manual gearbox for the 225bhp quattro.

In order to keep this power under control, the TT Roadster quattro has six forward gears and power transmission to both axles. This makes it, apart from the Lamborghini Diablo Roadster, the world's only open-top, two seater with permanent four-wheel drive.

Audi also offered in some markets from 2001 a new version of the 1.8T four-cylinder turbo engine. This unit developed 150bhp at 5,700rpm. This power still accelerates the TT Roadster from 0 to 100km/hr (0–62mph) in 8.9sec and on to a top speed of 214km/hr (134mph). The engine has a usefully flat torque curve (154lb ft from 1,750 to 4,600rpm), providing ample pulling power. So, although 0–96km/hr (0–60mph) takes another 0.3sec, the Roadster still feels as fast as the Coupé. Not only that, these turbo engines delivered a good fuel economy for the performance they provide: the TT Roadster is rated 22mpg in town and 30mpg on the highway (12.84 and 9.42ltr/100km); the values for the quattro are 20 and 28mpg (14.12 and 10.1ltr/100km). The quattro version, by spreading power among all four wheels, is better balanced through corners. But it weighs 136kg (300lb) more than the front-drive model, so it does not feel so wieldy.

Roadster Control

Like the TT Coupé, the Roadster was compact, with a short wheelbase, wide track and large wheels that fill its wheel arches. It has a low centre of gravity, with firm shock-absorber and spring ratings that play their part in achieving optimum stability on the move, and McPherson struts with anti-roll bars at the front. For some drivers though, the Roadster has so much weight and activity

Here is why the Roadster feels so solid and scuttle-shake free. Reinforcement was a priority for Audi's engineers and it shows in this detailed cutaway.

upfront that it could feel rather a handful. Too much power too soon, and the front-drive Roadster tugs at the steering wheel and runs wide through bends.

The rear axle design varies according to the model, of course. Front-wheel-drive cars have a compact torsion-crank layout, which, by means of its track, camber, toe-in and suspension settings, is ideally prepared to cope with any sporting activity. The more powerful TT Roadster with quattro driveline was equipped with a relatively unsophisticated rear end comprising a trailing-arm and double-wishbone rear suspension. It also minimizes encroachment on the available space and ensures magnificent roadholding. Both rear-axle versions include an anti-roll bar, which reduces body roll to a minimum when cornering rapidly. Overall, Audi softened the dampers by 10 per cent because of the cruising character of the Roadster, but this is not noticeable.

Shake Free

Scuttle shake, rattle and roll have spoilt the enjoyment and dynamics of many convertibles over the years. Remove the roof and the structure starts to shake. Remember, though, that Audi designed both the TT and the Roadster in tandem and built much rigidity into the structure.

The superb torsional rigidity of the Roadster is due to the substantial design of the side sill sections. Their size and special profile and the use of reinforced steel make a major contribution towards avoiding any significant vibration, even when you are travelling over rough surfaces. As well as the sills, the dash panel mount with the massively reinforced window frame above and the two leather-padded aluminium supports below, also contributes significantly to rigidity. The two supports form a solid bridge between the centre console and the transmission tunnel. The A-posts incorporate two interlocking tubes made of high-strength steel, which run from the highest point to multiple joints on the floor-pan assembly.

In bottom-line terms, torsional rigidity reaches 7,353lb ft/degree, which equalled a Porsche Boxster and almost matched a Lotus Elise's 8,088lb ft/degree. Inevitably, the reinforcements bring the kerb weight from

1,395kg (3,070lb) to 1,475kg (3,245lb) for the 225bhp version. The natural body frequency is 22Hz. Compared with the Coupé, the mass is up, but at 40kg (88lb), not by as much as might have been expected. Audi says that the Roadster has a 'massive portal frame structure' behind the seats, which constitutes a link between the floor assembly and side panels of 'extreme torsional stiffness'. There is also a rectangular aluminium crossmember, which makes a flexurally stiff mounting for the car's twin roll-over bars. Indeed, the roll-over bars can impose loads of up to 3.2t (3.5 ton) to the structure without any noticeable deformation, according to Audi. All these reinforcements to the body have been designed with the aid of computer simulations, with the result that vibration has been reduced or eliminated entirely. So no steering wheel shake, gear lever wobble nor scuttle vibro massage.

Research has shown that for these results up to 100kg (220lb) of extra weight would normally have been incurred. Audi engineers were able to undercut this computed limit by 60 per cent. Nevertheless, it helped make the Roadster one of the safest places to be in in the event of a crash.

Safety Bars

Indeed, Audi believes that the Roadster unlocks a new chapter in open-top car safety. The most distinctive safety features are the two aluminium roll-over bars which, with a gleaming matte finish, not only represent a striking, slightly retro design feature, but also form an integral component of the body structure and a major contribution to the Roadster's safety and structural rigidity. Occupant protection in the TT is not limited to those bars. Other safety features include crumple zones at the front and rear, high-strength, side intrusion protection bars in the doors and large-volume body sill sections.

There is also a sturdy windscreen frame with a double anchorage inside the A-posts, additionally reinforced by a high-strength, steel tube-in-tube system. Two front airbags for driver and passenger and pyrotechnic seat belt tensioners combined with belt-force limiters are all part of the TT Roadster's standard equipment in Europe, as are the side airbag systems integrated into the seat backs and designed to protect the head and thorax. The car's body meets European legal side-impact (96/27/EC) collision requirements effortlessly, and, in fact, already fulfils future European frontal impact standards (96/79/EC).

After the Coupé's high-profile, high-speed accidents (*see* Chapter 7), active safety in the TT Roadster became a major issue. The standard equipment includes an electronic stability program (ESP) including electronic differential lock (EDL), electronic brake-force distribution (EBD) and all-speed traction control (ASR). This system enables the driver to remain in control of critical situations when approaching the handling limits. The space that the large 16 or 17in rims provide has been fully utilized to install large brake discs. Along with the anti-lock brake system, large (312mm front and 232mm rear) ventilated brake discs are used on the front wheels and the 225bhp TT Roadster quattro has them (239mm) at the rear, as well.

There are additional reserves of driving safety and dynamics, because of the uprated sports suspension with its wide track. The front axle uses the tried and tested McPherson strut principle. The rear axle on the quattro version has a trailing arm and two wishbones at each side, with separate spring and shock absorber mountings. On front-wheel-drive cars, compact torsion-crank rear suspension with precisely tuned elasto-kinematics ensures accurate wheel location.

Slip Inside

It is cosy inside a Roadster, but visibility is at a premium, since it is poor to the rear and the sides, because the convertible-top design, headrests and roll-over bars mar sightlines to the rear and sides. In the cockpit area particular attention has been paid to every detail, as in the TT Coupé. The sports steering wheel, the dashboard instruments with matte aluminium surrounds, and the pedals and the stainless steel support for the footrest all have what must now be regarded as typical TT design details. From the satin-finish instrument panel trims to the leather-covered, padded supports at the right and left of the centre console, the gear knob and – outside the cockpit – the striking fuel tank filler cap, it is all very TT.

In addition to these, there were several features designed for extra comfort and convenience inside the Roadster: high-grade leather seat upholstery, central locking with remote control, plus various compartments for smaller items located in the rear panel behind the seats and protected by the central locking system. The side sections of the Roadster's sports seats are upholstered in leather, with Alcantara used for the central panel. The 'baseball glove' leather, which was an impressive feature of the design study, was also available on request in the production Roadster as part of the optional, authentic package. As well as the conventional seams, the

You can never stare for long enough at the superb Roadster interior. Here is a 2002 model with full optional package.

sections of the seat are 'threaded together' by a leather tape. According to Audi, this recalls the way the American Indians bound their moccasins. And to ensure an ideal driving position, the TT Roadster driver could vary the position of the three-spoke, leather-covered steering wheel axially and vertically. However, the seats themselves are fairly stiff and tight, with limited height adjustment. To get into the right driving position may be difficult for some.

It did not merely look good in there, it sounded good too. That sonorous 1.8ltr engine could roar provocatively when provoked. Otherwise, switching on the 'Concert' radio allowed the 225W output from the Bose Sound System to flood the Roadster's cockpit with sound, which meant perfect reproduction from the four loudspeakers integrated into the doors and the additional ones, including sub-woofers, behind the seats. However, the controls were fiddly and com-

plicated. But at least the cup holders did their job well, although some might complain that they would have to reach backwards.

For the majority of markets there was state-of-the-art theft protection. The Roadster had an electronic interior monitoring system that uses a pulsed radar effect to monitor for intrusion, even when the roof is lowered. Another part of the interior was the boot; it was not huge, but the 0.22cu m (7.8cu ft) of space there is certainly enough for a weekend's worth of soft luggage.

The new Roadster rear luggage rack for the Audi TT model has solved a logistic problem: how to carry skis and snowboards. The new lightweight rack, made of chrome-plated steel, can be installed when the soft-top is closed and also secures the skis and snowboards against theft when they are attached to the car. An additional rear brake light is integrated into the rear tube of the rack to maintain safety even in difficult winter driving conditions.

Audi was proud of the cubbyhole quotient on the Roadster and there was still a decent amount of room in the boot.

Not so Aerodynamic

Open-top cars always suffer aerodynamically as turbulence, eddy currents and various small or larger interruptions to the airflow all affect the drag coefficient much more than in the case of an enclosed, fixed-roof vehicle. Clean-cut, breakaway edges are not always available, and large air inlets at the front to supply a turbocharged engine with the necessary combustion and cooling air intensify the conflict facing designers and aerodynamic engineers.

Audi wanted minimal air resistance and lift, but with no negative influence on styling. This meant that no prominent spoilers could be used to guide the airflow, which may have turned out to be a major mistake (*see* chapter 7). Instead of putting the spoiler on top of the car, it was positioned underneath. The result: a drag coefficient of 0.36 was thought by Audi to be an extremely good result for a roadster. Actually, it is not, especially when compared with the Porsche Boxster at 0.31. However, when the hood on a Roadster is dropped it becomes 0.39.

At least the Roadster is quiet. When driving with the soft-top raised, even at high speeds, wind noise remains low. This is due to the fine-tuning of the design, including the position of the mirrors, the rigid rear window and the soft-top sealing. The height of the windscreen, the shape of the soft top, the position of its struts and even the weave and tension of the cloth were designed so that the airflow remains in contact for as long as possible and the cloth is subjected to a minimum of turbulence. This also prevents the soft-top from billowing out at high speed.

With the top down, even greater aerodynamic advantages come to the fore. In spite of the less effective airflow afforded by the low windscreen typical of a roadster, the interior of the car still has a pleasant microclimate. The radically new design of windbreak, available as an optional extra, further reduced airflow effects inside the car. Hood up or down, the TT Roadster was every bit as good as the TTS indicated it would be. Great to look at, good to drive and extremely well built, the Roadster was the perfect complement to the TT Coupé, but what did the press really think?

TT Roadster Specification			
Vehicle type:	front-engine, front-wheel-drive, 2-passenger, 2-door roadster, 180bhp with 5-speed manual transmission and front-wheel drive, /quattro all-wheel drive; 225bhp with 6-speed manual transmission and quattro all-wheel drive	**Engine** **Type:**	front-mounted, transverse, in-line, 4-cylinder with 5 valves per cylinder, turbocharged, charged air intercooling
		Displacement:	1.8ltr (1,781cc)
		Bore:	80.8mm
		Stroke:	86.4mm
		Compression ratio:	9.5:1/9.0:1
Body/chassis:	2-sided, fully galvanized steel construction, multi-step, anti-corrosion protection, aluminium bonnet	**Cylinder block:**	cast iron
		Cylinder head:	aluminium alloy
		Valvetrain:	DOHC, belt-driven and hydraulic lifters

Firing order:	1-3-4-2
Fuel injection system:	ME.7.5 Motronic(r) with electronic multi-point sequential fuel injection, hot film air mass sensor, solid-state direct ignition with multiple coils, dual knock sensors with cylinder selective knock control, electronic throttle operation, fully adaptive controls
Emission system:	heated oxygen sensor, activated charcoal filter, 3-way catalytic converter

Performance

Horsepower (SAE net):	180bhp @ 5,500rpm/ 225bhp @ 5,900rpm
Torque:	173lb ft @ 1,950–4,700rpm/ 207lb ft @ 2,200–5,500rpm
Acceleration (seconds):	0–60mph: 8.0/7.7 quattro/6.7
Top speed:	224/219/242km/hr (140/137/151mph)
Combined fuel consumption:	26/23/23 mpg

Transmission

Type:	5-speed manual with synchronized reverse, dual mass flywheel and hydraulic clutch
Gear ratios:	1st: 3.300:1/3.818:1/3.417:1; 2nd: 1.944:1/2.105:1/2.105:1; 3rd: 1.308:1/1.345:1/1.429:1; 4th: 1.034:1/0.972:1/1.088:1; 5th: 0.838:1/0.970:1/1.097:1; 6th: /0.912:1; reverse: 3.938:1/4.630:1/4.107:1

Steering

Type:	rack and pinion, variable power assist
Ratio:	15.6:1
Turns (lock-to-lock):	2.8
Turning circle (curb-to-curb):	10.4m (34.2ft)

Dimensions

Wheelbase:	2,422/2,429mm (95.4/95.6in)
Track:	1,525/1,513–1,525/1,507mm (60.0/59.6–60.0/59.3in)
Length:	4,041mm (159.1in)
Width:	1,856mm (73.1in)
Height:	1,346mm (53.0in)
Weight	1,420/1,550/1,575kg (3,124/3,410/3,465lb)
Weight distribution front–rear:	61/39–58/42
Luggage capacity:	221/181ltr quattro (7.8/6.4cu ft)

Suspension (uprated in 2000)

Front:	McPherson struts (gas-charged) with 3-point lower control arms, directly coupled stabilizer, negative roll radius
Rear:	torsion-beam axle with trailing arms, stabilizer bar, separate coil spring and shock absorbers (gas-charged), toe-correcting axle bushings
Rear, FWD:	torsion-beam rear axle with trailing arms, separate coil spring/shock absorbers (gas-charged), stabilizer bar and toe-correcting axle bushings (on 180bhp models only)
Rear, quattro:	parallelogram multi-link independent, coil spring/shock absorbers (gas-charged), stabilizer bar, electronic stabilization program (ESP)

Brakes

Type:	dual diagonal circuits with anti-lock braking, vacuum-power assist, asbestos-free linings, electronic rear-brake pressure proportioning
Front:	12.3in (312mm)/12.3in (312mm) ventilated discs
Rear:	9.1in (232mm)/9.4in (239mm) diameter solid discs/10in (256mm) ventilated discs

Wheels/tyres

Wheels:	7J × 16-cast aluminium, 5-spoke design/7.5J × 17 6-spoke design
Tyres:	205/55 R16/225/45 R17, space-saving temporary spare

Capacities

Engine oil:	4.5ltr (4.75 US quarts)
Fuel tank:	55ltr (14.5 US gal)

Standard features

Exterior

- heated glass rear windscreen
- 2 fixed roll bars with polished aluminium finish
- manually-retractable top or power folding top with heated glass rear window standard according to market
- power outside mirrors with defog feature
- heated windshield washer nozzles
- body-contoured, 3-way headlight assembly with ellipsoid low beam and foglights, polycarbonate lenses
- 2 front foglights
- high-pressure, retractable headlight washers

Interior

- 3-spoke, leather-wrapped, sport steering wheel with aluminium centre trim ring
- leather-wrapped shift knob and hand-brake lever
- manually-adjustable tilt-and-telescopic steering column
- interior lights in headliner, with fade-in and fade-out feature, time delay, and automatic activation when key is withdrawn from ignition
- illuminated glove box, trunk, lighter, ashtray
- fully automatic, climate-control system with sun sensor, dust and pollen filter
- power windows with power retention, 'one touch up, one touch down' and pinch protection
- radio-frequency, remote locking system with selective unlock, remote boot opening, panic function, interior lights and alarm system activation (control integrated in folding ignition key)
- power central-locking system (doors, trunk, and fuel door), with selective unlocking (enables unlocking of a single door or both doors), plus convenience open and close features for windows
- retained accessory power after key is removed from ignition
- front sport seats with manual height adjustment
- nappa leather seat upholstery, including door panel inserts
- aluminium trim on centre dashboard vents, shift lever knob and base, knee bolsters on centre console, door release handles, radio cover, glove box cover
- 4 tie-down eyelets in rear cargo area
- 2 aluminium cupholders in centre console
- tool kit located in rear storage compartment of rear cargo area
- seating capacity: 2

Safety

- anti-lock brake system with electronic differential lock and electronic rear brake pressure regulation
- driver and front passenger next generation front airbag supplemental restraints
- driver and front-seat mounted chest and head side airbag supplemental restraints
- front, 3-point safety belts with automatic pre-tensioning and force limiters
- central locking system with safety unlock feature (if airbag deploys)
- emergency warning triangle located in rear cargo area
- first-aid kit
- fixed head restraints

Electronics/instrumentation

- illuminated backlit instrument cluster with automatic brightness control, including tachometer, electronic speedometer, digital clock with date, service interval indicator, fuel and coolant gauges
- driver information display with 5-function trip computer including outside temperature and radio/telephone displays, active auto-check system with speed warning device and pictogram display for open door and trunk/deck lid

–   anti-theft alarm system with blinking theft-
    deterrent light
–   windshield wipers with 4-position adjustable
    intermittent interval rate

Audio

–   120W Audi Concert AM/FM stereo with CD,
    Radio Display System (RDS), Graduated Audio
    Level Adjustment (GALA), CD changer operation
    capability
–   pre-wiring for 6-disc CD changer
–   rear-mounted radio/telephone antenna

Options

–   global positioning Audi navigation system

–   power folding top (standard on some models,
    according to the market)
–   Amber Red baseball-optic leather interior
–   unique 'nubbed' TT cloth upholstery with leather
    bolsters (no-cost option)
–   17in, 5-spoke forged alloy wheels with 225/
    45 tyres (225bhp model)
–   17in, 6-spoke cast alloy wheels with 225/45 tyres
    (180bhp model)
–   Bose 225W, premium 8-speaker sound system
–   6-disc CD changer
–   heated front seats with individual temperature
    control
–   xenon high-intensity discharge headlights with
    automatic self-levelling

6 On the Street

The fabulous TT Roadster proves once more that Audi has its finger on the pulse of the time. It's a sensational looking car, it oozes quality and style, it's an absolute joy to drive, and it's surprisingly economical to buy and run.

Car

After the international motor showrooms, public relations puffery and admiring glances, the TT now had to survive and, most importantly, prosper in the real world. That meant that the TT would have to meet its toughest critics in the shape of the press and also a marketplace that was starting to brim with coupé and roadster rivals. So the question was: how did it actually drive?

TT vs. the Rest

Car magazine did what any decent publication would when they got their hands on the all-new TT coupé: pitch it against similar products on sale in Europe at the time. In this case and in the October 1998 issue it came up against the Mercedes SLK 230K and the Alfa Romeo GTV V6 24 V. The BMW Z3 Coupé did not count because it was available only in M-trim and cost rather more. They immediately observed that the TT was a two plus no one taller than 1.5m (4ft 11in) in the back, as a warning sticker on the B-post warned. Never mind, it was a four-wheel-drive sort of four seater, versus a rear-wheel-drive, two-seat roadster/coupé and a front-wheel-drive, four-seat coupé. A mixed bunch then, but it was

certainly possible to judge the difference between them.

Car said that it was almost impossible not to be impressed by the Audi's stylish and functional interior. It believed that 'every switch, every lever feels solid and practical, the ergonomics are simply faultless, and the materials are unashamedly worthy of a car two or three times the price'.

When it came to driving the TT hard *Car* made some important discoveries in the light of the controversy that would later surround the car's handling. Discovering a 104km/hr (65mph) downhill right-hander with a constant radius and smooth surface, the TT lapped it up, holding its line in one progressive motion. Taking the same route in the other direction up the incline at 112km/hr (70mph),

Halfway through the bend, just past the apex, you can feel the torque split as the Haldex clutch starts feeding power to the rear wheels. The steering gets lighter as a result of the weight transfer, the tyres begin to protest, and during the final quarter of the curve, at an indicated 75mph [120km/hr], the rear end commences a slow-motion slide that requires a hand's breadth less lock. No drama. No sweat. No need for wild corrections.

Although the engine was, on paper, the most powerful, it was not perfect. *Car* did not think it was smooth enough, that the turbocharger and wastegate were at odds with each other, and that there was erratic high-speed, high-

The view from the TT cockpit; Car magazine gave the thumbs up to the ergonomics and practicality and said that the quality was worthy of car two or three times the price.

rev throttle response. However, they still found that it was willing to rev, with low noise and plenty of low-end torque that worked well with both the clutch and the transmission.

Car concluded,

The newcomer from Ingolstadt simply has the edge in all the important disciplines. The quality is terrific. The design is a milestone. The engine still needs some fine-tuning, but it does perform well against the stopwatch. The handling and road holding qualities are fit to make the competition pale. The TT is fun without punishment. Even at the limit, where steering angle, slip angle and throttle angle battle it out, you always know where you are and how the car will react. After all, this is the first quattro capable of understeer, four-wheel drive and oversteer. So it's a compelling drive. And it wins. With ease.

Old vs. New

Probably one of the most interesting comparisons was carried out in November 1998 in *Evo* magazine, in its first issue. It bought a 1990 20V Audi quattro and took it for a drive with an Audi TT for company to Italy via Germany. As it rightly pointed out, the question was not whether the real TT beat its closest rivals, or compared with a Mercedes SLK or a Porsche Boxster: what everyone really wanted to know was just how close the TT actually got to the original quattro.

Picking up the test TT in Germany, the periodical noticed that the biggest immediate contrast was the interior, 1980s angularity against 1990s design details. As for the driving experience:

> Where the quattro is a dynamic slow-burner, the TT is sharp and immediate . . . the quick, direct steering working with the pointy front-end to give the TT a sharp, aggressive feel. Actually it feels like a well-gummed-down hot hatch . . . In terms of sheer pace the TT is remarkably close to the quattro. Both are extremely quick when you stoke them up, but it's the quattro that delivers more entertainment.

The quattro had a genuinely characterful, five-cylinder engine, whereas the TT's unit was just a little bland. It was even considered then that a V6 would be the answer to give the TT a much better soundtrack. The conclusion was quite accurate, pronouncing the

The TT making a splash; Car magazine said that this was the first quattro capable of understeer, four-wheel drive and oversteer, which made it a compelling drive.

Audi quattro coupés, old and new. Evo found the TT to be sharp and comparable to the old 20V quattro. However, the older car was designed with no compromise and gave the purer peformance.

TT as a fabulous car, which was polished, entertaining and very well sorted. In short, no disgrace to the quattro badge. However,

> Where the old car scores over the new is in its engineering integrity. The quattro was a bespoke car, designed without compromise. The TT can't escape its underpinnings, but that's not to say Audi hasn't done a brilliant job of maximising its potential. Where the quattro was created by technical revolution, the TT is the result of clever product evolution. It's still not quite as polished or satisfying as the quattro, but the TT has earned the right to stand alongside its towering forebear.

Second Best

Autocar's Peter Robinson test drove the TT coupé twice and was very impressed. He described the engine as being both refined and tractable in low speed, then pulling strongly from 3,000rpm. Its tremendous torque at a wide rpm band aided in-gear acceleration and thus effortless driving. In addition, the gearshift was accurate and precise. That Haldex four-wheel-drive system, combined with the new rear suspension, would even enable a controlled power slide under hard cornering, but with lots of grip. Indeed, the body stayed flat, the brakes were powerful, while the ride remained supple. But bringing a Porsche Boxster into the picture was always going to prove to be the ultimate test.

It was noted that the Boxster did not have the acceleration of the TT. Clearly the 204hp/181lb ft, which the Porsche had on tap, was way behind the TT's 225hp/206lb ft, not only that, the TT had an additional gear ratio and the advantage of four-wheel drive's grip when cornering. Despite those important factors, Robinson preferred the Porsche 986: 'Audi, for all the cleverness of its engineering and the brilliance of its styling, is subtly compromised by its origins. The Boxster is a purer, more sharply focused and sensitive sports car.' He thought that the TT felt bulkier to steer, lacking the directness and feedback of the Boxster. The mid-engined Porsche also proved much easier to handle on the limit, with a sharper turn-in, excellent body control and ride. He also preferred the character of the flat-six to the turbocharged straight four.

Second best to the Boxster for many road testers, but just as nice to look at and in revised post-2000 specification, with suspension modifications and rear spoiler, even safer on the limit.

Robinson concluded that 'the Boxster is a better, more talented driver's car, a pedigree sports car that is simply more desirable even than the spectacular Audi'.

In many ways it was unfair to match a pure-bred, mid-engined sports car with 911 (996) heritage up against a platform-sharing exercise from the VW group.

First Best

'Cool, fast fun to drive – meet the topless German that has even the Boxster beat' is how *Car* magazine introduced the TT Roadster on the cover of its September 1999 issue. Thus proving that everyone had an opinion. It went even further, suggesting that:

The 225bhp Roadster is the perfect four seasons car. Subjectively it even beats the 911 Carrera 4 cabriolet, which is 130 per cent more expensive, but perhaps only 30 per cent ahead on ability. While the superb Audi 4wd system ensures optimum traction on all surfaces, the folding top offers optimum weather protection. Equipped with a heated glass backlight, it fits beautifully and provides almost as much insulation as a tea cosy.

73

Car loved the TT's quality, it even said that, with the exception of Bentley, no other car manufacturer devoted the same attention to detail, to materials and to craftsmanship. Getting back to the Porsche 911, it observed that, even though it cost less than half as much, the Audi looked more precious and felt even better made. It loved the way it drove too. Although the turbocharged four cylinder would lack the refinement and instant bottom end response of a six cylinder, 'this high-revving, all or nothing, five valve unit fits the character of the car. Of course, the TT quattro offers unbeatable grip and traction.' Interestingly, it found that the front-wheel-drive version was more predictable on the limit and much more fluent to driver inputs, meaning that it would not surprise a driver with sudden power oversteer or abrupt lift-off tail slide. Its conclusion was that:

> the fabulous TT Roadster proves once more that Audi has its finger on the pulse of the time. It's a sensational looking car, it oozes quality and style, it's an absolute joy to drive, and it's surprisingly economical to buy and run. You would have to spend a fair bit more money for a comparable Z3, SLK or Boxster, and that extra dough would not necessarily buy a better automobile, or one that would give you more pleasure.

The Audi TT Roadster not exactly pictured on the limit, but obviously in its digitally-enhanced element. Fun to drive, but, most importantly of all, even more fun to pose in. An attention-seeking bullet of a roadster.

Roadster vs. the Rest

After a year of familiarity, the novelty of the TT has worn off, replaced by an ever increasing fondness and attachment. Call us suckers for style, but the TT's beautifully sculpted and trimmed interior simply makes us feel good about the car every time we turn a wheel in it.

That was *Car and Driver*'s opinion and it is hard to disagree. It also thought that the coupé was practical enough, with a decent sized hatchback and room for a couple of 'third graders'. The quattro powertrain proved particularly adept at keeping the TT on the road all year round. Despite the arrival of the 225bhp version, it found the 180bhp 'peppy' enough and, although the Roadster was also available, it had a preference for the tin-topped model.

However, when *Car and Driver* pitched the TT Roadster against its main rivals, the Audi had more of a struggle. Facing the TT was the Mercedes SLK320, the uprated Boxster and the BMW M roadster. Of these the TT came only joint third, but in most areas the Roadster still registered bonus points. As a traffic-stopper and pedestrian jaw-dropper the TT beat all the other roadsters. This 'simply has to be the most interesting interior on the planet', said the road test team, although the roof leaked during a car wash, which was not so appealing. In handling terms, though, the now spoilered Roadster betrayed its Golf-based roots. It was pointed out that the roadster's weight distribution, even with its quattro all-wheel-drive system, was 58.7/41.3, in contrast to that of the rest of that group, which was closer to 50/50. And as regards weight, the Roadster tipped the scales at a considerable 1,561kg (3,438lb), by far the heaviest in the group. However, it found the six-speed manual transmission very slick and returned an impressive 0–60 time of 6.2sec, which matched the Boxster's performance.

In summary, *Car and Driver* felt that this was no focused sports car, with too many compromises that included its total weight, biased to the front, ride-oriented suspension, turbo lag and four-wheel-drive understeer.

Best Engine

In 2002 *Auto Strassenverkehr* pitched the TT against its close rivals, judging their merits purely in terms of engine output and performance. It observed that both the Mercedes SLK 320 and the Honda S2000 2.0i produced more than 200bhp. Mercedes relied on engine capacity, Honda on high engine speeds and Audi on a turbocharger. It concluded that the TT's technology was better because the turbocharger allowed for a smaller engine, which saved weight and fuel and enhanced driving performance. It thought that the 1.8ltr engine's 225bhp/380lb ft was not only impressive, but also delivered the power in the broadest and most effective manner. The future, it said, belonged to engines such as the TT's.

Long Term

The TT was not just a short-term fling for some magazines, but a long-term commitment. *Auto Motor und Sport* subjected an Audi TT Roadster to a tough 100,000km (62,100 miles), long-term test. Its verdict in 2002: Audi's designers had come up with a 'funmobile', with styling that had taken the wind out of its rivals' sails. The car subjected to the test was a 1.8T quattro with a 225bhp, four-cylinder engine. Throughout the test there was high praise for the good seats, which were comfortable and provided plenty of lateral support. The soft-top was also approved of: it generated little wind noise, even at high speeds, although it had no lining. At the end of the test the soft-top was still in good condition and sealed as well as ever. The engine

Audi TT at speed; it was generally well reviewed and four years later, despite a mid-life crisis, still rated as a long-term sporting companion. This is a 2002 US specification 225 quattro.

was a lusty puller and made every journey great fun.

Also in 2002 *AutoZeitung* issued an interim report on its Audi TT Roadster and observed that, thanks to its all-wheel drive, the 225hp Audi TT could be driven away even on snow-covered hills, with ESP and ABS to protect it against skidding sideways in uncertain driving situations. Initially, the fuel gauge was found to be inaccurate, but this was rectified under the warranty. All in all, the pleasure of driving the Audi TT could be described as consistently high after having covered 75,000km (46,600 miles) in it.

So the press gave the TT coupé and Roadster the thumbs up, but that was not the end of nor even the whole story.

7 Ingolstadt . . . We Have a Problem

And for those who remember the sensationalist press last year, I can tell you from expert personal experience, the TT has always handled quite superbly!

Anonymous, retired Formula 1 driver

For a while in the late 1990s it seemed as though the German motor industry could do nothing right. First there was the Mercedes A class that famously failed to negotiate a rather obscure Scandinavian test which involved avoiding an elk at speed. The A Class fell over. Unfortunately, it was captured on camera by a motoring magazine, so this became a high profile issue. Mercedes could not afford to hush it up, but went about re-engineering their new car and effectively relaunching it with the maximum amount of publicity. This incident even sent Mercedes back to the drawing board of its joint-venture MCC Smart car that it also discovered could handle trickily if provoked. Installing traction control was the answer there. The point is, that in the current consumer climate a car company that expects its research and development programme to be finished for it by the buying public is going to get into trouble. So why was Audi not paying attention?

Full or Fool Proof

Perhaps it did not realize that products these days have to be utterly full and also fool proof. If people buy high-performance sports cars they expect to be able to use them as such.

They also expect that any skill deficiency should be taken care of by the on-board technology. In the TT's case that would be ABS brakes and the majority of the models that have the Haldex four-wheel-drive system. Certainly the TT was deliberately set up to give a fairly sharp lift-off oversteer (getting the tail out) so that it was reactive, just like a generation of hot hatches such as the Peugeot GTi.

The first hint of trouble was a report by the German magazine *Auto Motor und Sport*. They carried out a comparison test where they pitted the TT against its close relatives in the shape of the Volkswagen Golf 4motion and the Audi S3. What they discovered was that high stability was questionable. It was not unreasonable to expect that a high-performance car generates a low aerodynamic lift, but the TT recorded 418/567N front and rear lift at 190km/hr (120mph) compared with the Volkswagen Golf's 19/340N. Audi chose to ignore these findings and then the crashes started.

In September and October 1999 two fatal, high-speed crashes happened in Germany and were extensively reported. Another German magazine *Stern* even interviewed many TT owners and published their experiences. After several more non-fatal crashes, Audi announced in October an offer to replace the suspension and install a rear spoiler at no charge to all TT customers worldwide. But with three more fatal crashes reported the following January, Audi stepped up the pace –

since not all the drivers could be said to be inexperienced, especially when the former East German road rally champion Peter Hommel crashed his TT and was killed. Audi said it investigated around fifty-five crashes, all of which, including the five fatal ones, occurred in Germany. And not only that, all the drivers were apparently pushing their cars past 175km/hr (110mph).

A case widely reported in the British press involved Chris Meek. His TT was just 16km (10 miles) old. Confronted by overtaking traffic coming in the opposite direction on a familiar road, he turned left, decelerated and touched the brakes. The road was dry, although there was a crosswind. The TT's tail came out, he corrected; it then swung the opposite way and the car snaked across the road, hit the offside barrier head on and rolled on to its roof while crossing back to the nearside. Meek unfortunately broke his neck while his partner sustained a fractured skull that was almost fatal.

Talking to *Car* magazine in January 2000, Meek said: 'I said at the time there was something wrong with that car.' Meek refuted any claim that he made excuses, having owned high-performance cars in the past. His own

investigations revealed that the incident was not unique in Britain. Even though the police estimated that Meek was travelling at 146km/hr (91mph), there was no prosecution.

Unspoilt

Yes, the TT coupé looked marvellous, but it seems that there was a triumph of style over the law of physics: those cannot be changed, but it was part of the design philosophy to ignore well-established aerodynamic principles.

Reading Audi's press releases over the last few years it is clear that it thought that it knew what it was doing: 'The tasks listed in the design specification were clearly formulated: minimized air resistance and lift, but with no negative influence on styling. This meant that no prominent spoilers could be used to guide the airflow.' It went into detail about how it avoided using a spoiler. Apparently a quarter-scale model was subjected to comprehensive tests in a water tank and the sharp edges, which are mainly responsible for turbulence, were designed out. Furthermore, in Audi's new wind tunnel the vehicle was positioned on a simulated moving road, placing the car on fast-

Audi put its faith in ground-effect technology to help keep the TT on the road. These underfloor panels were designed to cut the aerodynamic drag by 10 per cent and to cut the lift at both axles. It was not enough.

moving belts that caused its wheels to rotate. A further belt passed beneath the car's body to simulate the road surface. It claimed that the knowledge gained about the airflow path permitted a solution that could not have been identified by conventional methods. This led directly to the spoilers being integrated into the underbody, so that turbulence at the large wheels was significantly reduced. It also meant that the additional air volume needed to cool a high-performance turbocharged engine was still achieved, together with a frontal area of only 1.99sq m (2.4sq yd). It claimed that the result was exceptionally low resistance to the airflow. Perhaps it should have carried out more real-world testing.

NACA

It put its faith in aviation industry principles. Audi said that its aerodynamicists had to work out how to supply the powerful engine with the necessary volume of cooling air, without spoiling the car's aerodynamics. The NACA air inlet was claimed to be the solution. This takes its name from the organization which preceded the better-known space authority NASA. So when the aerospace engineers had to develop new cooling concepts for aircraft, in other words, to divert as large a volume as possible of air into a suitable duct in order to cool the engines and the oil, the best solution was found to be an aperture which increases in width according to a special pattern – a technique used on racing cars. Racing cars, though, also have very visible spoilers. NACA inlets are used on Audi models in the engine enclosure panels underneath the car, and on the TT a nose-end enclosure improves the airflow in the front axle and engine areas, while a large fuel-tank cover panel performs the same function at the rear. Eddy currents round the wheels are smoothed by spoilers integrated into the underside of the body.

Under normal driving conditions this system worked very well. There are low levels of wind noise at high speeds in the TT. Indeed, it is very snug in there. Special door seals, for example, prevent resonance from building up in the panel and door cavities. The frameless side windows generate only a minimum amount of wind noise right up to the car's top speed. Like many similar designs to ensure that the doors can be shut without undue effort, despite the side windows pressing firmly against their seals, the windows move down by about a hand's width whenever the door handle is operated and slide back up again after the door has been closed.

Unaerodynamic

Audi certainly had an enviable record in slippery and effective shapes. In 1982 the Audi 100 set up a new aerodynamic world record for saloon cars, with a drag coefficient of only 0.30. Certainly the engineers seemed pleased enough with the drag coefficient of 0.34, which must be one of the highest recorded in the last decade for a sports car. That brings us to the *Auto Motor und Sport* findings on the TT's lift quoted earlier.

Ideally, the TT would need a basic teardrop shape because it naturally causes the least disturbance to the airflow around it. The Honda Insight follows this principle and actually tapers from front to back, such that the rear wheels are 10.9cm (4.3in) closer together than the front. That is acceptable for an economy car, very bad for a sporty one, but the intention is the same: smooth airflow. However, because even smooth airflow over a teardrop shape eventually separates into turbulent flow, the body's line needs a cut-off. Known as a Kamm tail, this allows the airflow to break cleanly and predictably from the body. In contrast, rounded bodies can have a flow separation point that moves around,

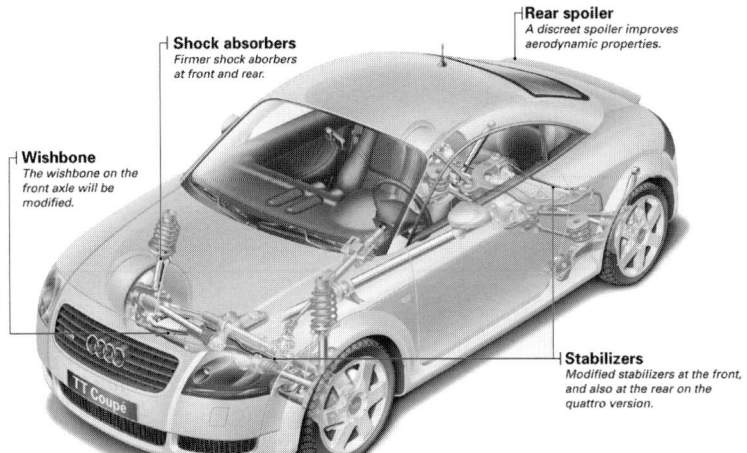

Rear spoiler
A discreet spoiler improves aerodynamic properties.

Shock absorbers
Firmer shock aborbers at front and rear.

Wishbone
The wishbone on the front axle will be modified.

Stabilizers
Modified stabilizers at the front, and also at the rear on the quattro version.

Here is what Audi did to make the TT handle better, no further explanation needed really.

Here is what Audi did to the Roadster, but in German for added dramatic effect.

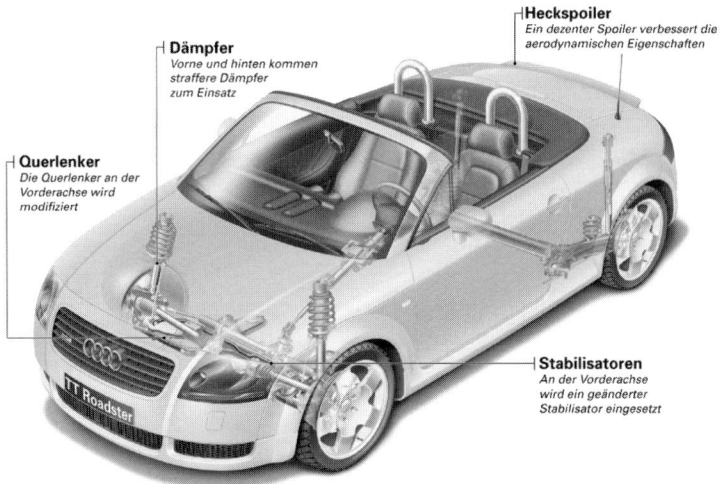

Heckspoiler
Ein dezenter Spoiler verbessert die aerodynamischen Eigenschaften

Dämpfer
Vorne und hinten kommen straffere Dämpfer zum Einsatz

Querlenker
Die Querlenker an der Vorderachse wird modifiziert

Stabilisatoren
An der Vorderachse wird ein geänderter Stabilisator eingesetzt

depending on conditions. That may cause handling changes, resulting in more lift and reducing grip at the rear wheels. So that is one possible reason why the TT became a little nervous on the limit and needed a spoiler to help out. So when the front end dipped under braking, the shape meant that the lift got more severe, emphasizing any lack of rear grip. What that meant was that at the speeds and in situ-ations where many drivers would want the car to be more stable (backing off during a high-speed bend, because it was getting sharper or there was a hazard to be avoided) the TT actu-ally became more tail happy.

It was no surprise that the Audi engineers finally admitted that they might have been wrong. Talking to the journalist Peter Robin-son in February 2000, Dr Bernd Heissing,

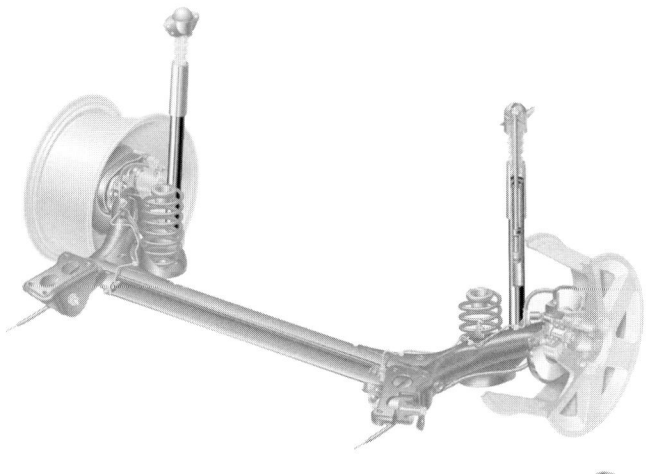

Modified stabilizers were fitted to the front suspension of front-wheel-drive models, and quattro versions had these stabilizers fitted both front and rear. A modified wishbone was fitted at the front, together with firmer damper settings at the front and rear.

Audi's head of chassis development, admitted, 'There was a lot of discussion during development, and we all decided not to include a spoiler. Now, we've changed our minds.' Another possible reason was that the relatively unsophisticated rear suspension was not doing its job.

Suspend Belief

Some drivers have noticed that the rear suspension has too much – or at least insufficiently controlled – travel, creating geometry changes which makes the tail feel wayward even at low speeds. Even the revised TT feels the same, but, by contrast, the Roadster is not that twitchy at all. It is structurally sound, but not as sound as the coupé and that extra give means that the suspension is more compliant and controlled. The German magazine *Zeitung Car* published a report which showed that, in normal conditions, the weight was distributed 60 per cent in front (885kg [1,956lb]) and 40 per cent in the rear (576kg [1,273lb]). However, braking at high speed, 80 per cent of the weight is located at the front (1,173kg [2,592lb]) and just 20 per cent (288kg [636lb]) at the rear.

Audi Acts

Audi announced a recall on all the 40,000-plus TTs sold in Europe up to that point. In summary, it would fit thicker anti-roll bars, firmer dampers and a rear spoiler. The front wishbone was also to be revised. The scheduled updates affected both the car's suspension and its aerodynamic performance. Modified stabilizers were to be fitted to the front suspension of front-wheel-drive models, and quattro versions would have these stabilizers fitted at both front and rear. A correspondingly modified wishbone would be fitted at the front, together with firmer damper settings at the front and rear. In addition to these suspension modifications, the TT would receive a rear spoiler.

According to Audi, the modified suspension settings and the rear spoiler would help the TT to retain its satisfying agility, while the limits of stability would be spread over a broader range, with the result that drivers would find the car easier to keep under control.

The modifications obviously became part of series production. Meanwhile, Audi requested that all TT owners bring their cars into a workshop to have them modified and additional components fitted free of charge. For production and logistical reasons, the after-sales measures were implemented in two phases: the suspension modifications would be carried out first, followed by the retrofitting of the spoiler. Once the necessary parts were available, Audi dealers would be able to perform the modifications for customers at short notice. 'Customer satisfaction has top priority for Audi', declared the Audi spokesman Rainer Nistl in Ingolstadt on 21 January 2000, 'For this reason, the retrofitting campaign for the TT is currently in full swing.' Nistl explained that Audi's accident researchers had been investigating incidents involving the TT from the very start. According to their findings, it was not possible to establish a pattern of accidents typical for the TT. One driver was killed on a notorious high-speed Autobahn curve. A second fatality occurred to an unbelted rear-seat passenger. Audi reported that its accident investigation group had studied twenty-two crashed TTs; that may sound like a lot, but given the number of TTs sold worldwide, the ratio of accidents to it is similar to that of other sports cars. Nistl stressed:

> For Audi, customer satisfaction also means settling the matter for TT drivers in conjunction with the dealer organization in a suitable manner that is acceptable to all parties . . . The Audi TT does not have any design defects. Many specialist publications have described it as particularly agile and as having excellent cornering ability, and it has been praised in countless articles and test reports. In the most recent issue of the well-known British automotive magazine *Car*, the TT was once again described as the 'best-handling affordable car of the year'.

However, the TT came in for more criticism for its stability limit, which, as is typical for sports cars, is 'narrower' than for saloons.

> Audi responded extremely quickly and comprehensively [declared Nistl]. Various changes to the suspension and a spoiler have modified the car's handling so as to render the limits of handling noticeable earlier on and make the vehicle easier to control. As the specialist press has reported: 'This finally puts the Audi sports car on the safe side . . . ' (*Auto Motor und Sport*, 12 January 2000).

Audi Apologizes

Audi quickly offered the owners of the TT the chance to have their vehicle retrofitted with the electronic stability program (ESP). This was announced by Dr Franz-Josef Paefgen, chairman of the Audi AG board, at a press conference in Munich. The announcement was a direct response to growing uncertainty among TT customers. Not only had this been provoked by criticism about the car's handling, but customers were also starting to worry that this would result in a considerably lower resale value for TTs without ESP. 'I wish to apologize formally to our TT customers for the uncertainty which has emerged in the last few months. Our offensive is intended to put an end to this uncertainty', declared Paefgen.

But not all his words were well received. Some thought that it was insensitive and inappropriate for the Audi chairman to say that

The only visible clue that this was a modified TT; the rear spoiler spoilt the lines, but added valuable down-force and therefore stability.

five deaths in TT coupé and Roadster crashes was not many simply because as many as 9,000 a year were killed on the Autobahns in Germany. Paefgen should have known that he should never say anything that makes death seem inconsequential.

According to him, the company has continued to work intensively on analysing the handling of the TT, at the same time looking for suitable solutions to satisfy customers. In order to provide an objective assessment of the car's handling performance, TÜV Süddeutschland (South German Technical Inspection Association) was commissioned to carry out a detailed inspection of the TT compared with its competition. TÜV's summary was: 'The Audi TT – including its original versions – is, compared with the competition, a better-than-average sports car and is in keeping with the state of the art.' The message was clear enough.

As Paefgen remarked, Audi was very satisfied with this result since it confirmed Audi's statements in their entirety. But customers' letters have made it clear that a satisfactory solution can only be found if ESP is retrofitted. Audi had always stressed that retrofitting work as complex as this was not technically

83

Cornering at speed and braking in corners were no longer worries, and the handling on this 2000 model quattro coupé is much more assured, say the experts.

possible at the workshops of dealerships. That was why an assembly hall was specially converted for this purpose at Ingolstadt. This allowed ESP to be retrofitted in accordance with Audi's own high technical and quality standards. All this activity was estimated to have cost the company some $75 million.

ESP Explained

In case you wondered, electronic stability program (or ESP) makes use of the ABS electronic anti-lock braking system and also incorporates the ASR traction control. Whereas ABS and ASR operate along the line of travel, ESP influences the lateral dynamics of the car. This is made possible by installing a yaw-rate sensor (yaw is the car's rotary movement around its vertical axis). If the car tries to turn more sharply into the corner (oversteer), ESP applies the brake at the outside front wheel before the tail can break away. By braking this wheel, a moment is generated to oppose the car's oversteer and keep it stable. The opposite is true in understeer or push

conditions where the driver turns the wheel and the car tends to maintain a straight path. ESP not only processes the yaw rate, but also the readings from a steering angle sensor mounted just behind the steering wheel, from a lateral acceleration sensor and from the four wheel speed sensors. From all these data inputs it compares the steering angle and the wheel speeds with the yaw and lateral acceleration rates and detects any departure from the desired values. It then determines where and to what extent the wheel brakes should be applied.

After Effects

The Audi press relations department then went into overdrive and on to a race track with an ex-Formula One driver. They went to the Laguna Seca raceway with Michele Alboreto in an Audi TT 180 quattro for several gruelling laps. When asked how he liked the car, Alboreto said that he felt the TT was '. . . very neutral and wonderful to drive.' No hint of instability on the track was detected at any speed and there was no suggestion of lightness or tendency to oversteer suddenly. But that response was probably only to be expected. The problem with that sort of demonstration was that they chose the 180hp quattro version of the TT, which is 24km/hr (15mph) slower than the 225hp version. Compared with the non-quattro version, its heavier rear end also helped the stability. Not only that, a race track will not re-create the conditions found on an Autobahn.

The TT's flaw was primarily a Germany-only problem, because that is the only country in Europe where it is legal to exceed 128km/hr (80mph). Audi said that the main aim of the changes was to increase understeer, reduce lift-off oversteer and improve high-speed stability. The modified front control arms had altered compliance in the mounting bushings. The front shocks were stiffer in compression and softer in rebound to reduce the pitch motion and weight transfer from the rear to the front under braking. The front anti-roll bar was been made 1mm thicker and the rear 1mm smaller in diameter.

The most obvious change was the small rear spoiler mounted to the boot lid, which was crucial in reducing lift on the rear axle at high speeds. So the TT had 148lb of lift at the rear axle at 200km/hr (125mph) without the spoiler, but only a 53lb lift when the spoiler was fitted. By comparison, the BMW Z3 coupé generates 64lb of lift at 200km/hr; the Mercedes-Benz SLK 104lb of lift; and the Porsche Boxster 68lb of lift. Interestingly, Audi chassis engineers claimed that they could have solved the problem without the spoiler, but this would have meant a significant increase in understeer at normal speeds, something they wanted to avoid.

Under Autobahn conditions, when switching lanes and braking at speeds of over 160km/hr (100mph), the tail was no longer wayward and stability was less of an issue. Anyone could now drive a TT confidently

and manoeuvre at speed with much more confidence. However, at slower speeds, magazine road testers found that it was the steering which showed up the changes. The altered suspension slowed the steering, so turn-in was much more gradual, which meant that more lock was required when cornering.

TT OK?

So is the TT an unsafe car? No, just an unlucky one. It was also a new car and therefore easier to blame. There is a legendary rear-engined German sports car which had notoriously tricky handling on the limit, although it was never recalled nor modified until recently. High performance cars can bite back, but the TT was never given the benefit of the doubt.

The TT accidents were due to excessive speeds at inappropriate times. The ex-rally driver Peter Hommel was travelling at 200 km/hr (124mph) on a secondary road. There are two ways of looking at this: either he was travelling too fast and unfortunately lost control, or if anyone could handle such a car at high speed it should have been him. So perhaps it was the car's fault. The truth probably is that sensible drivers should know their limits and practise restraint. 'Driven by instinct' was the international advertising line for the TT, and, although you could take it in a number of ways, most of us instinctively know when we are driving beyond our limits.

Four-wheel drive is only an aid to traction and is no guarantee that a car will remain stuck to the road. Drive round a tight corner at speed and backing off the throttle inevitably causes problems, as it would with any car. The weight shifts forward and to the outside of the direction of travel, pulling the rear and nearside tyres away from the surface and then you have a spin. You could blame the car, but in the majority of cases it has to be the driver's fault. The modifications were good publicity, but what Audi should have done from the beginning was to fit a spoiler. Design purity prevented that, but then it is only truly effective at the highest of speeds.

If you are unlucky enough to have an accident in a TT at least it is a safe place to be. It achieved top five-star ratings in front-impact tests in the US National Highway Traffic Safety Administration passenger safety crash tests. The front-impact tests measure the effect of a 56km/hr (35mph) crash on dummies in the driver and front-passenger seats. Side-impact tests measure the impact of a 62km/hr (38.5mph) collision on a driver and a rear passenger. Among ten vehicles examined in the 2002 side-impact crash tests, the Audi TT convertible won the only five-star rating, for the driver's side.

Car was often quoted as giving the TT the thumbs up to the original, unmodified model. Again, they may have been thrashing the TT around a circuit rather than on an Autobahn, but they never noted any twitchiness. In their 1999 Performance Car of the Year assessment they said:

> The ride is firm to the point of being crashy when the road surface turns lumpy. The steering is direct, and the wheel is a very satisfying thing to lay your hands on . . . Regardless, for your £30K (with change) the whole package comes together in a way that allows you to push it about vigorously at speed. I found it especially lip-smacking on a series of tight uphill switchbacks on a rain-slicked stretch of the A40 [a road in England]. I could feel how the drivetrain was helping me; the only things more firmly stuck to the road than the TT were the cat's eyes.

Then, of course, there was the Formula One driver who insisted on remaining anonymous in this book. I shall quote him because these comments about the TT were in the public domain.

Audi, of course, is synonymous with four-wheel-drive technology and that is exactly what the TT has to ensure that the 225bhp can be firmly transmitted to the tarmac, rain or shine, through a slick, six-speed, manual gearbox. The grip and stability afforded by the 4WD system simply has to be experienced to be believed – it is phenomenal. And for those who remember the sensationalist press last year, I can tell you from expert personal experience: the TT has always handled quite superbly! Part of the fun is discovering the forte of each car. The TT's traction, cornering on hard acceleration, is quite extraordinary.

More Trouble?

After the embarrassment and cost of sorting out the TT's handling difficulties, it then seemed to attract an unfair number of recalls and controversy concerning several components. Audi voluntarily recalled forty-six 2000 Model TTs in the USA to correct a potential problem with the fuel lines. It then discovered that, in some TTs, a small section of the fuel line assembly, which is attached to the underside of the vehicle, could have been damaged during production. If damaged, the fuel line could leak to the outside of the vehicle and potentially cause a fire. There were no owner complaints attributed to this concern nor have there been any fires, accidents or injuries. Audi, however, was aware of one occurrence of leakage involving a company-owned vehicle.

In February 2001 it was replacement tyres for TT and S4 owners, even if the tyre damage was due to potholes. An Audi spokeswoman said that Audi took the unusual step after receiving complaints from several owners about tyre sidewall bulges and blisters causing loss of tyre pressure. Dealers would replace the affected tyres, which are size 225/45R-17/91Y that came as original equipment on 1998 and 1999 S4s and 2000 and 2001 TTs. Significantly, no accidents have occurred as a result of the tyre problem.

The 2002 British-specification TT that caused trouble by offering more for less, whereas the S-Line launched in late 2001 offered more, for much more, and was supposed to be a limited edition.

In late 2001 it was discovered that the ball joints in the rear trailing arms of the Audi TT quattro manufactured before March 2000 were prone to corrosion due to the failure of a lubricant applied during manufacture. The failure resulted in the ball joints becoming stiff, and causing energy to be transferred to the trailing arms, resulting in possible fracture. So all four trailing arms (upper and lower) were replaced with improved parts, including improved ball joints. The parts were redesigned in that the original design was reinforced.

Audi also had some difficulty in the United Kingdom in 2002. It promised to hand back up to £2,750 to 200 TT buyers whose 'exclusive' S-Line cars turned out to be less than exclusive. Marketed as 'exclusively assured', each £30,350 S-Line had 18in alloy wheels and lowered sports suspension, a specification that for the 2002 model year became standard anyway. That meant a 225bhp TT cost £3,600 less than the S-Line, and the 180bhp version some £6,300 less. An Audi spokesman said, 'UK sales of the TT have been so good we could have reduced the price but we chose instead to add equipment and preserve the residual values of existing cars.' The specification change apparently cost the company £500,000.

8 Getting Better

. . . relaxed driving experience . . .

Audi launch the 150bhp
entry-level engine . . .

the automatic transmission is a welcome alternative for drivers who prefer convenient, carefree shifting.

. . . and bring in automatic transmission

Give or take the odd subsequent major worldwide recall, the TT was very nearly perfectly formed when it emerged into most markets in 1999. So how do you improve on perfection? Well, there are always going to be technical improvements that will make cars more fun, more comfortable or simply more affordable.

Less Power

To fulfil the sales target (which was set so high because of the high development cost), Audi needed a stripped-down version of the TT. In certain markets it was important to make the TT more accessible and Audi had just the engine for it. Already used in the A3 and Volkswagen's Golf GTI, among other group products, the 150bhp (110kW) version of the 1.8ltr, four-cylinder turbo was offered in the Roadster and coupé from 2000.

Developing 150bhp at 5,700rpm, it managed to accelerate the TT Roadster from 0 to 100km/hr (0 to 62mph) in 8.9sec and on to a top speed of 214km/hr (134mph). Audi said

that it had taken account of the wishes of numerous convertible enthusiasts who particularly enjoy driving an open-top vehicle in a relaxed style: cruising along smoothly rather than changing gear hectically with a lot of footwork. It could well be right, when the whole point of so many open tops is to pose rather than to perform.

Audi also reckoned that the firm, sporty suspension satisfies the driver's every wish as far as dynamism is concerned. And not forgetting the engine's flat torque curve (154lb ft from 1,750 to 4,600rpm): this provides the basis for ample pulling power, and thus the driving style preferred by so many Roadster drivers.

In Germany, sports seats were standard with TT upholstery cloth. Alcantara and leather upholstery, the leather package authentic and heated seats could all be ordered as options. The extensive range of standard equipment included 'luxury' details, such as electrically-adjustable and heated door mirrors, electric windows and a three-spoke, leather-rim, sports steering wheel. The open-top Audi is fitted with 16in cast aluminium wheels of five-arm design. Obviously the comprehensive safety package includes the electronic stability programme (ESP) as well as front and side airbags for both occupants.

Three-Shaft Six

In some markets the six-speed gearbox became standard equipment on the 180bhp

This is a coupé with just 150bhp, although there is no way of telling unless you can peek under the bonnet.

model within a year of launch. With this unit, fifth, sixth and reverse gears are transmitted by way of an additional, third shaft. One advantage of this gearbox is that it occupies less space than a conventional, two-shaft design, but is capable of transmitting high torques – up to 257lb ft. As a weight-saving measure, magnesium is used for the casing. Gears are selected by a wire-cable mechanism. This has the advantage that no rigid mechanical linkage is present between the gearbox and the gear lever, so that the transmission of vibration is largely avoided. Features include a short lever travel, a direct gear-change action, well-defined selection points and a precise clutch.

Auto Hit for Six

For 2003 the 180bhp coupé and Roadster models now featured the FrontTrak front-wheel-drive system and a six-speed, automatic transmission, marking the first application of an automatic transmission in the TT. The six gears result in improved performance, with the gear ratios closely matched to the engine's performance characteristics.

The 180bhp model has a peak torque of 173lb ft at 1,950–4,700rpm, and features Tiptronic steering-wheel-mounted gear shifting controls. The front-wheel-drive coupé, with six-speed automatic transmission, has a 0 to 96km/hr (0–60mph) time of 7.9sec, while the 180bhp Roadster accelerates from 0 to 96km/hr in 8.1sec.

Contributing to the TT's performance for 2003 are optional, 17in, all-season tyres for both the 180 and the 225bhp engine models. For TT coupés and Roadsters with the 225bhp engine, exclusive 18in, all-season tyres are also available. All cast-alloy wheels, regardless of size, are updated for 2003.

Seven-spoke, 16in cast-alloy wheels are standard on 180bhp models, while 225bhp models feature standard six-spoke, 17in cast-alloy wheels with concave spokes. Optional on the 225bhp models are seven-spoke, 18in cast-alloy and five-spoke, 17in forged-alloy wheels.

New Look and Specification

Although the TT has never even needed a mid-life make-over, there were a few subtle

The new 2003-model TTs sports a bolder grille and some vibrant colours.

detail changes for 2003 models: an aggressive new grille with vertical and horizontal cross sections and the trademark Audi four rings, as well as new polished-chrome 'TT' badging in a sleek design to match the body. Other 2003 highlights include distinct exterior accents, new colour combinations for the TT Roadster and purposeful interior refinements.

Both the 2003 TT coupé and TT Roadster have a standard New Generation Audi concert stereo with in-dash CD player and an optional enhanced Bose sound system, with AudioPilot noise compensation technology. All 2003 Audi TT and A4 models feature AudioPilot, a noise-dampening system that continually filters interior and exterior noise and adjusts for better music quality in real time. The coupé and Roadster also feature the available HomeLink universal remote transmitter, and this year will offer four new exterior colours: Brilliant Red, Ocean Blue, Goodwood Green and Dolomite Gray. Inside, all versions of the 2003 Audi TT coupé have fine nappa seats, with door panel inserts standard. The coupé also has two new interior colours: Ocean Blue and Vanilla, while the TT Roadster adds Vanilla and Black Baseball Optic to its interior colour palette.

90

TT 150 Specification

Vehicle type: front-wheel drive, 2-passenger, 2-door roadster and 4-passenger coupé, 150bhp with 5-speed manual transmission

Body/chassis: 2-sided, fully galvanized steel construction, multi-step anti-corrosion protection, aluminium bonnet

Engine

Type: front-mounted, transverse, in-line 4-cylinder with 5 valves per cylinder, turbocharged, charged air intercooling

Displacement: 1.8ltr (1,781cc)

Bore: 81.0mm

Stroke: 86.4mm

Compression ratio: 9.5:1

Cylinder block: cast iron

Cylinder head: aluminium alloy

Valvetrain: DOHC, belt-driven, hydraulic lifters

Firing order: 1-3-4-2

Fuel injection system: ME.7.5 Motronic(r) with electronic multi-point sequential fuel injection, hot film air mass sensor, solid-state direct ignition with multiple coils, dual knock sensors with cylinder selective knock control, electronic throttle operation, fully adaptive controls

Emission system: heated oxygen sensor, activated charcoal filter, 3-way catalytic converter

Performance

Horsepower (SAE net): 150bhp @ 5,700 rpm

Torque: 154lb ft @ 1,750–4,600rpm

Acceleration (seconds): 0–60 mph: 8.5; top speed: 213km/hr (133mph)

Combined fuel consumption: 28mpg

Transmission

Type: 5-speed manual with synchronized reverse, hydraulic clutch and traction control ASR

Gear ratios: 1st: 3.300:1; 2nd: 1.944:1; 3rd: 1.308:1; 4th: 1.034:1; 5th: 0.838:1; reverse: 3.938:1

Steering

Type: rack and pinion, variable power assist

Ratio: 15.6:1

Turns (lock-to-lock): 2.8

Turning circle (curb-to-curb): 10.4m (34.2ft)

Dimensions

Wheelbase: 2,422mm (95.4in)

Track: 1,528/1,513mm (60.2/59.6in)

Length: 4,041mm (159.1in)

Width: 1,764mm (69.4in)

Height: 1,349mm (53.1in)

Weight (Roadster): 1,335kg (2,950lb)

Weight distribution front–rear: 61–39

Luggage capacity: 221ltr (7.8cu ft)

Suspension (uprated in 2000)

Front: McPherson struts (gas charged) with 3-point lower control arms, directly coupled stabilizer, negative roll radius

Rear: torsion-beam rear axle with trailing arms, separate coil spring/shock absorbers (gas-charged), stabilizer bar

Brakes

Type: dual diagonal circuits with anti-lock braking, vacuum power assist, asbestos-free linings, electronic rear brake pressure proportioning

Front: 12.3in (312mm) ventilated discs

Rear: 9.1in (232mm) solid discs

Wheels/tyres

Wheels: 7J × 16-cast aluminium, 5-spoke design

Tyres: 205/55 R16, space-saving temporary spare

Capacities

Engine oil: 4.5ltr (4.75 US quarts)

Fuel tank: 55ltr (14.5 US gal)

The V6 in action. It has purposeful styling with a deeper front spoiler and an extended rear lip, which helps keep the V6 firmly on the tarmac. Audi claims that the TT's DSG transmission can cope with anything from edging away smoothly on an icy surface to full throttle starts.

Audi TT customers in many markets could now choose the optional Premium Package, which includes heated front seats with individual temperature controls, HomeLink universal remote and self-levelling, xenon high-intensity discharge headlights.

An 80W, six-speaker system with in-dash CD player is standard in the TT coupé, while a 120W system with an additional speaker between the seats comes standard in the TT Roadster. For concert-quality sound, Bose Music Systems are optional and deliver 175W in the TT coupé and 225W in the TT Roadster.

Audi 3.2 V6

Some said that the TT finally got the engine it deserved and also the innovative high technology edge that defines the modern Audi. So in December 2002 Audi unveiled the first version of its TT coupé sports car to feature a 3.2-litre six-cylinder engine and completely new transmission technology. The combination of the well-proven and high-torque 3.2-litre engine developing 250bhp and an innovative sports gearbox powering all four wheels led to a vast improvement in the car's already remarkable performance.

The new TT V6 still has the familiar high-quality cockpit, which is beautifully constructed and finished. The only clues that this is the 3.2 are the new shift surround for the DSG gear lever, the paddles behind the steering wheel and the speedometer that reads up to 175mph.

The truly revolutionary Direct Shift Gearbox (DSG as Audi call it), co-designed with Borg Warner, is designed to combine all the benefits of a conventional six-speed manual gearbox with the qualities of a modern automatic unit. It operates in a similar way to Ferrari's F1 system, supporting both automatic and manual shifting with the aid of the gearlever or shift paddles behind the steering wheel. The driver is supposed to benefit from enormous agility, driving enjoyment and economy as well as convenient operation and smooth acceleration with, most importantly, uninterrupted traction. Porsche were apparently so impressed with the system that they have considered adopting it.

V6 TT'd

The power was provided by Audi's well-known 3.2-litre V6 engine, which was suitably modified. It was a good choice because, with its cylinder angle of 15 degrees, it is extremely compact and is therefore especially suitable for installation transversely to the direction of travel. Also, the valve-control process generated marginal friction thanks to the use of roller cam followers with hydraulic adjustment.

Other technical details such as continuously adjustable inlet and exhaust camshafts and the variable intake manifold give the six-cylinder engine superior torque and power output, coupled with low emissions. A great deal of detail work has been invested in this area in particular, in order to further improve its peak output and torque characteristics. The engine now delivers 250bhp (184kW) and has a broad peak-torque range with a maximum value of 236lb ft (320Nm) from 2,800 to 3,200rpm, whilst the compression ratio is 11.3:1. Significantly, the TT V6 has 22bhp and 29lb ft more than the 225 TT, with only a few kilos more in weight.

Throttle valve actuation is designed for an exceptionally agile, spontaneous engine response to accelerator pedal movements. The way it interacts, particularly with the ultra-rapid, precise-control technology of the new twin-clutch transmission, opens up an entirely new dimension in propulsive power.

The sound of the dual-branch variable exhaust system suitably reflects these sporting characteristics. A flap in the exhaust system is opened or shut depending on engine speed. Its sonorous sound never becomes over-

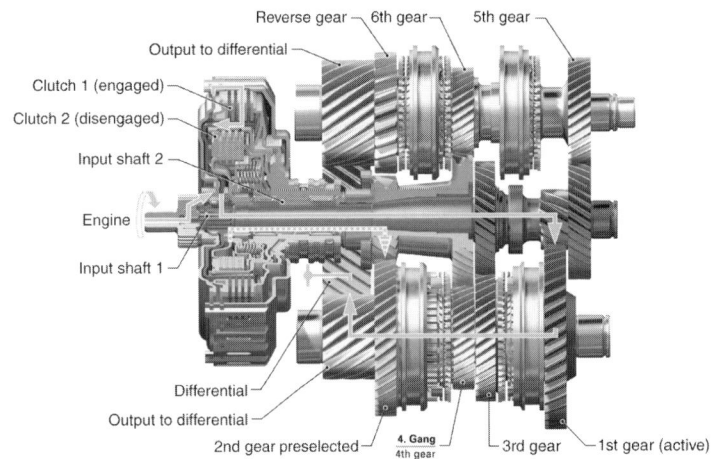

Reverse gear — 6th gear — 5th gear
Output to differential
Clutch 1 (engaged)
Clutch 2 (disengaged)
Input shaft 2
Engine
Input shaft 1
Differential
Output to differential
2nd gear preselected — **4. Gang** 4th gear — 3rd gear — 1st gear (active)

Here is what happens in first gear and (below) when second is engaged. The DSG gearbox is novel for its compact twin-plate clutch, which enables the next gear to be used to be pre-selected, offering the potential for much quicker shifts. Electronics deduce which gear will be required next, while the hydraulically controlled clutch has been programmed to cope with different shift styles and strategies. Suddenly moving away from rest smoothly, the bane of many a paddle-shift sports car, has been solved.

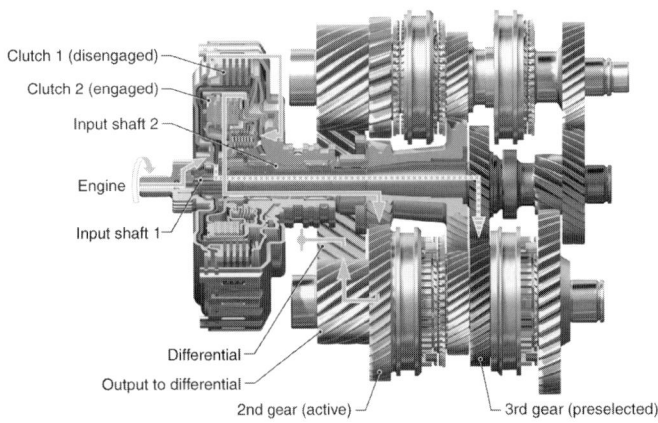

Clutch 1 (disengaged)
Clutch 2 (engaged)
Input shaft 2
Engine
Input shaft 1
Differential
Output to differential
2nd gear (active) — 3rd gear (preselected)

assertive, even at high engine speeds, yet it unmistakably conjures up all the sentiments that sports-minded TT drivers appreciate. Yes, there is a great sports-car soundtrack as the note builds along with the revs up until the red line. Back off at 5,000rpm and there are the crackles and bangs of unburnt fuel trying and failing to escape from the exhaust. The turbo models sound very tame by comparison.

The Audi TT 3.2 accelerates from 0 to 100 km/h in just 6.4 seconds, whilst the top speed is gently governed at 250km/h (155mph). Provisionally the overall consumption is around 28.8mpg (9.8ltr/100km). The differences compared with the conventionally geared automatic transmission with torque converter are even more impressive, since the latter is prone to significantly higher transmission losses due to its fundamental concept. So let's find out just how this revolutionary new gearbox works.

DSG Explained

The basis for the new development is a six-speed manual gearbox with high variability in the selection of the transmission ratio. Thanks to the use of an integrated twin multi-plate clutch with an ingenious control system, two gears can be engaged at the same time. During dynamic operation of the car, one gear is engaged. When the next gearshift point is approached, the appropriate gear is preselected but, crucially, the clutch is kept disengaged. The gearshift process opens the clutch of the activated gear and closes the other clutch at the same time. The key is that the gear change takes place under load, with the result that a permanent flow of power is maintained. This technology may be unique on a road car, but it is not exactly new. The first time that the world saw a twin-clutch transmission was in 1985, when Walter Röhrl successfully tested such a system in his Audi Sport quattro S1.

For the 2003 model year the new design satisfies the exacting requirements of convenient gear-shifting and maximum operating life for everyday use. This transmission has been developed at group level and is built at the Kassel transmissions plant. This compact transmission is capable of handling torque of up to 245lb ft (350Nm).

Operating DSG

The electronic control unit integrated into the transmission casing maintains optimum gearshift strategies that perform lightning-fast gearshifts that are nevertheless smooth and almost jolt-free. The driver can directly influence the gear selected and the gearshift timing at will, by means of the gear lever in the manual gate or the standard-fit shift paddles on the steering wheel.

In the automatic mode, the driver can shift from position D to the ultra-sporty S pro-gramme, in which upshifts are retarded, downshifts advanced and the shifting process accelerated. In addition, a remote one-touch function accessed via the shift paddles on the steering wheel temporarily calls up the manual mode even in automatic modes D and S. High overall efficiency is thus combined with superlative road performance and ease of control. The user interface is reminiscent of the familiar gearbox gate of the Audi tiptronic or multitronic.

If all that sounds frighteningly complicated, in practice the DSG transmission is very easy to use. Start the engine and make your first choice: manual or automatic? In manual there is no clutch pedal, you simply change gears by nudging the lever up and down. Alternatively you can work the shift paddles behind the steering wheel. When the TT stops, the computer automatically selects first gear. Hitting the red line will automatically trigger an upshift.

When in automatic mode there is another set of choices, either D for drive or S for sport. In S mode it shifts down very early and shifts up at the rev limiter. The real party trick is the launch control feature. With ESP switched off, one foot on the brake and the other on the accelerator the TT V6 takes and then revs all the way to 6400rpm before changing. There is also a noticeable blip of the throttle when it downshifts. Obviously position D is set for comfort with a smoother shift action at lower revs. Overall, though, the DSG system is seamless, delivering uninterrupted high power.

So is DSG perfect? Pretty much, although it cannot anticipate every driving condition. When, for instance, you need to suddenly accelerate to overtake and the gearbox has decided to go for a higher gear: you will have to wait almost a second for DSG to adjust. Some road testers have suggested that the actuators can be felt doing their stuff changing gear ratios. That is nit-picking, though, because the DSG is as near as any manufacturer has yet got to building the perfect transmission system.

Packing the High Tech in

As on conventional manual gearboxes, the transmission ratios are present on input and auxiliary shafts in the form of pairs of toothed wheels. In contrast to manual gearboxes, the input shaft is divided into two sections: an outer hollow shaft and an inner shaft. The 1st, 3rd, and 5th gears, and reverse, are located on the inner shaft. The hollow shaft handles the even-numbered gears.

Each of these shafts is selected by means of a separate multi-plate clutch running in oil. The two electronically controlled, hydraulically actuated clutches are packed inside each other for maximum space economy. As well as

their high efficiency and ability to transmit high torques, clutches of this type permit a wide range of starting characteristics. In other words, the multi-plate clutch can be controlled in such a way that every conceivable form of pulling away is possible, from an ultra-gentle edging along on a slippery surface to sports-style acceleration at full throttle. The gearshifts it produces feel spontaneous and decisive, as if executed at the push of a button. The electronic-control throttle blip feature of the manual and S modes reinforces the impression of ultra-dynamic gearshifts.

In the upper section of the transmission casing is housed the 'mechatronic' shift-by-wire control system, which combines hydraulic and electronic control units. The signals from ten individual sensors are processed centrally there, and the actuation

A six-speed sequential semi-automatic gearbox is not a new idea, but at least Audi got their first back in 1985 with the Audi S1 quattro.

A 2002 TT Roadster in full UK specification.

Hood up, the TT Roadster looks and is as purposeful and snug as the Coupé.

left
A Brands Hatch instructor's 225 TT, which is not modified in any way for the track, apart from the racing tyres.

below
Cooling down after their hot laps at Brands Hatch, these are the instructors' cars at the racing school.

opposite *Roadster and Coupé in perfect harmony.*

What a sight: more than twenty TTs (some out of shot) waiting for their lucky pupils at Brands Hatch.

A 225bhp Roadster waiting to entertain under a bright, if cloud-filled sky.

Superb quality and detailing – it can only be the cockpit of a TT Roadster.

Picture perfect – a 225 TT under a cloudy, but blue, sky.

One of the TT's most distinctive design features, the brilliant fuel filler cap.

There is not a lot to see under the bonnet of a TT but, like the rest of the car, it is still very neat.

The Coupé cockpit is snug and ergonomic: every nicely detailed control falls perfectly to hand.

You can get a surprising amount in that flat load bay of the TT Coupé.

A wonderful view of the TT Roadster, showing the alloys, angles and radius to full effect.

Not a bad boot for an open-topped car, the TT Roadster can certainly 'do' luggage.

Even the TT door trim is a subtle design masterpiece.

Early design sketches, but unmistakably a TT.

The original TTS, first seen in Japan in 1995.

The gorgeous interior of the TTS; it was not surprising that virtually no major changes were made to this cockpit.

values calculated using the relevant information on the momentary driving situation from the drive CAN bus. The application pressure of the two clutches is regulated by special solenoid-operated valves depending on the situation, and the gear positioners operated.

The electronics also calculate which additional gear is to be preselected by the corresponding positioning cylinder and selector forks, and manages all actuating elements and the oil cooling circuit via six pressure regulation valves and five on/off valves.

All in all, the entirely new concept results in a decidedly agile performance, with the added benefit of the typically low fuel consumption of an advanced six-speed manual gearbox.

Handling the Power

A 17in dual-piston brake system adapted from the version used on the RS 4 gives an appropriate braking performance. There are floating-caliper brakes with ventilated brake discs, 334mm at the front and 265mm at the rear. This set-up is hugely effective and pedal feel is much improved over the original model's, appearing to deliver much shorter stopping distances. In common with all TT models, the new 3.2 quattro has ESP with integral brake assist. However, some sporty drivers may feel that the electronic stability programme interferes too early, but after Audi's experience with high-speed stability it is not surprising that they have programmed the system for caution.

The body sits a little bit lower than standard, on a MacPherson strut front and multi-link rear set-up, which has been fitted with stiffer springs, uprated dampers and slightly thicker anti-roll bars. That means that the ride is still firm on smooth surfaces, but body control and overall balance are improved, so in the middle of a corner there is plenty of control to match the grip. Grip is not an issue

as the large 225/40 section tyres help keep the TT V6 on the road, although it is possible to provoke some tail movement by backing off mid-corner. The power-assisted rack-and-pinion steering, already very direct at just 2.6 turns between locks, has been improved. Many accuse the original TT of having a numbness and detached feel: this has been addressed and is certainly sharper than before.

The dynamism of the new top-of-the-range TT version is also demonstrated in the car's outward appearance. The main changes compared with the other TT models are the modified rear spoiler and the front apron with enlarged inlet openings and lateral gills. The larger rear spoiler further reduces rear-end lift, in line with the performance gain of the TT 3.2 quattro. The front apron now incorporates larger openings to cover the higher demand for cooling air, without the aerodynamic properties being affected. The drag coefficient remains unchanged at a disappointing Cd = 0.32.

The TT 3.2 quattro, in addition, has xenon lights as standard with range control and titanium-coloured headlight trims. Inside, as well as the shift paddles on the steering wheel, this version is distinguished by a gearbox gate in polished aluminium and an instrument panel insert with a speedometer extending as far up as 280km/h or 175mph.

Sum Up

Many wonder why it took Audi so long to put such a characterful engine under the TT's bonnet. After all, it is VW Golf-based and there has been a V6 option on that model, although engineers regularly made the excuse that there was not enough room for a larger powerplant. What concentrated the corporate minds must have been the imminent launch of the six-cylinder Nissan 350Z, a revised Porsche Boxster, a new BMW Z4, the Mercedes SLK and the radical Mazda RX-8.

With V6 power the TT has a new lease of life: this is the view that many of its rivals will have to get used to.

So just when critics were thinking that the TT was getting on a bit, Audi do the clever thing and reinvent the model, making it more desirable and sporty. The V6 injects performance, refinement and real character. An uprated chassis, more aggressive styling and a very clever gearbox have given the TT a new lease of life.

9 Construction

The TT assembly line at Györ was in operation six days a week, to cope with the high level of demand as Audi aimed to reduce TT delivery times down to six months.

– Audi realize that they have a
hit on their hands

Building cars in two different locations is often a recipe for disaster, or at least major quality problems. The Hillman Imp had its body pressed in Coventry and was then put on a train and later finished off at Linwood in Scotland. Here was an innovative car let down by indifferent assembly. The Dual Ghia had a body built in Italy and then finished in America. Financially that made the project falter. So why did Audi think they could build the TT both at Ingolstadt and in Hungary and get away with it? The motor industry has moved on a long way since the 1960s and 1970s, it really is an international business. Overseas partnerships are an integral part of the automotive economy and Audi already had a state of the art engine plant at Györ in Hungary.

Construction began in November 1992. The new engine plant was officially opened less than two years later. A workforce of around 4,900 was employed there at the start of 2001. Audi has access to a good supply of

The completed bodies are carefully prepared for painting.

An independent logistics company removes the painted TT bodies from specially-designed rail cars after they had travelled overnight from Ingolstadt.

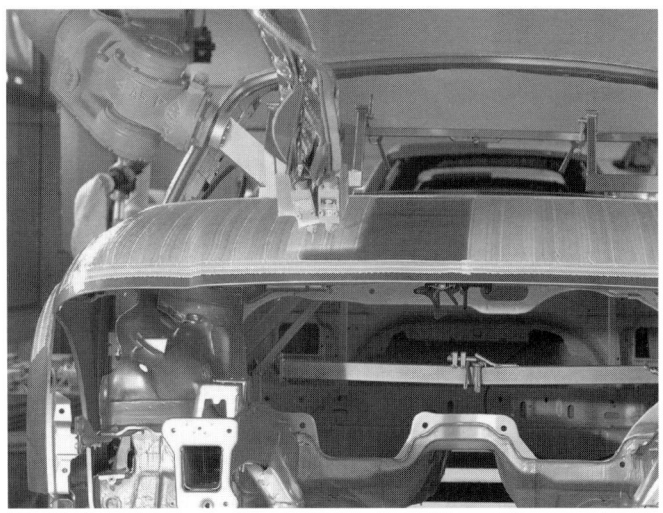

Once painted, a spray-on film of aqueous polyester–polyurethane dispersion is applied by robot (not pictured).

skilled workers and highly qualified graduates from the Institute of Technology. Staffed by a highly trained workforce building the A3's powerplant, Audi Hungaria's main business is actually producing engines, not building cars. It is the only remaining Audi engine plant and produces four-, six- and eight-cylinder engines for all of the Volkswagen group

divisions – a million engines in total each year. It was therefore logical to use the existing facilities for something rather more ambitious. It also helped that the Hungarian government had conferred on the industrial area a duty-free status that meant generous tax breaks and lower assembly costs. Logistically it would all work because the rail companies ensured that the infrastructure would be in place. That is why the completed body shells leave Germany in enclosed freight carriages and overnight are delivered right inside the Györ factory.

600 kilometres

The story of the TT's construction begins some 600km (380 miles) away from Audi Hungaria, in Ingolstadt in Bavaria. The stamping of the TT body panels, welding and paint-work are executed in Germany. That means Audi Hungaria Motor Kft is responsible solely for assembling the parts and for maintaining quality control.

Two hundred new TTs leave Ingolstadt daily. In the precision body shop Audi uses two laser welding cabins. When the production plants were planned, this reliable and tested technology was deliberately chosen. Following the positive experience with optical-fibre technology for the A3 body construction, this was also chosen for INTERBUS networking in the Audi TT control system. The system was

planned by Audi AG in Ingolstadt. the plant supplier for building the underbody and body lines was Krupp-Drautz GmbH of Heilbronn. The lines required to produce the bootlid were supplied by the welding system manu-facturer Kuka Schweissanlagen GmbH of Augsburg. Audi itself provided the production lines for side panels, doors and hoods.

What Audi are committed to building is the strongest bodywork structures possible which are crucial to the dynamics of the TT coupé and the Roadster. Even chassis engin-eers will admit that body rigidity is a decisive factor when it comes to delivering precise handling and road-holding. That means that the running gear needs a substantial body structure against which to 'react': even in the most severe conditions there must be no dis-tortion. Body movements generate oscillation, which can conflict with the movements of the suspension and have an adverse effect on the car's road behaviour. So the TT coupé achieves the high torsional rigidity required with roof frame and door sill elements with a very generous cross-section – up to a third

The finished Audi TT shell begins its 240-metre journey along the Gyor assembly line.

Györ's speciality is building the turbocharged 4-cylinder engine.

larger than in comparable saloon cars, though in practice little heavier. The dimensions and patterns of the elements that connect the body sections together are also of decisive importance. On the TT coupé, for instance, the door sills are anchored to the front and rear roof posts and the rear side members by means of large-area metal sections in the side panel frames. Inside, the distinctive struts to the left and the right of the centre console which look so good actually strengthen the entire area between the dash panel and the floor pan, and in doing so significantly reduce steering wheel shake.

Scientifically, high levels of torsional and bending strength are essential if vibration and body shake are to be minimized. The TT coupé therefore achieves outstanding results in this area. Engineers will tell you that its static torsional rigidity is 14,000lb ft (19,000Nm) per degree of angle and the first intrinsic bending frequency is as high as 50Hz. Which means that this is a rigid bodyshell with a clean vibration pattern. On the road, that translates into a safe, comfortable, if firm ride typical of the TT.

Superb Finish

The exterior bodywork of the TT is finished with a coating system based on Bayer raw materials. First of all, polyurethane/epoxy binders based on Bayer's aromatic polyisocyanates are applied by cathodic electrodeposition. This gives the fully galvanized body added corrosion protection. Then a surfacer is applied to level out any irregularities in the substrate. For this, Audi has gone for water-dispersible (low-solvent) systems based on polyurethane coating raw materials, such as Bayhydrol and Bayhydur, which give a tough, flexible, but still sandable polyurethane film. This undercoat effectively protects the body from flying stones and improves the covering property of the pigmented base coat.

The final step is the application of a two-layer top coat. For the clear coat, Audi selected a high-solids, two-pack polyurethane system

The complete powertrain and chassis are installed in the body by lowering the body from overhead.

based on Desmodur. The polyurethane finish has excellent chemical and light stability and particularly good resistance to acid rain. Apart from this, it has outstanding scratch and stone-chip resistance and also retains its gloss and brilliance for many years. Fully painted TT bodies, with doors, are shipped via rail from the body/paint shop in Ingolstadt to Györ, a journey of around 12 hours. Special rail cars were developed to carry the bodies without damage; 90 per cent of the materials delivered to Audi Hungaria go by rail, most of which come from a consolidation centre in Germany that receives shipments from Audi's suppliers and then distributes them, as needed, to facilities throughout Europe.

On go the alloy wheels. The TT is almost ready though the seats have yet to be installed.

TT by the Cartload

The unloading of the train cars, the moving of the bodies into the plant and within are subcontracted activities. The TT bodies are wheeled into the plant on what are effectively carts or trolleys. Here they begin their journey down the 240m long, U-shaped assembly line where they will stop off at sixty-five separate stations and finally emerge as fully formed cars. Both coupé and roadster models travel down the same line. The carts/trolleys are used only in the initial stages. An overhead gantry system scoops the bodies up soon after the doors are removed and carries the bodies down most of the rest of the line. The line loops back on itself so that it actually begins and ends at the same distribution area.

In order to make a TT it is first dismantled rather than assembled. The doors are removed and then placed on stands, which are then wheeled down a subassembly line. On this, they are fitted with trim and accessories before they rejoin the body on the main line. All of the subassembly lines at Audi Hungaria

operate in this way. They actually run at right angles to the main line so that subassembly build ends immediately at the point where the part goes into the vehicle. The next major subassembly, the instrument panel, is put together and installed in the same way.

TT Trimmed Out

Looking much more TT-like, the cars continue down the line and, as they approach the bend, workers take parts from the line-side 'marketplace' to trim out more of the interior. At the same time, on a subassembly line located around the bend, another group of workers perform the precision work of assembling the engine, transmission and suspension parts. This is where the procedures become more complicated, because the TT is available in several combinations, especially as the front-wheel and four-wheel drive versions have different rear suspensions.

The powertrain/chassis assembly takes place on a parts jig that moves down a chest-high assembly line. This saves the workers from having to stoop or reach overhead. Once the parts are in the jigs, workers move them on top of an automated guided vehicle (AGV) by means of an overhead lift-assist. The AGV moves about 8m across an aisle to the main assembly line, where the car is now elevated in the gantry. The AGV slides underneath the car and the powertrain/chassis is bolted into the body. The AGV then returns, with fixtures, to the subassembly line.

Now that the TT has an engine, the assembly work on sundry under-bonnet components begins as the battery and airbox are added. Fascias are attached, both front and rear; lights, protective wing liners and the wheels and tyres are installed. Once the car has its wheels, it is set down on a four-pedestal conveyor for the seats to be installed. These are wheeled in on racks and immediately followed by the racks with the doors. This completes the assembly process and the cars are driven off the conveyor through a wash and inspection before they are covered and prepared for shipment back to Ingolstadt.

Lean Workers

There is much skilled hand assembly involved in building a TT – the installation of rear window glass in the coupé and the cockpit brace and roll bars in the roadster. One explanation for this is the relatively low cost of labour in Hungary. But there is more to it than that because it is true to the lean production principles adopted by the plant. Without too much automation, to adapt to the differences between the coupé and the roadster is therefore relatively easy. Indeed, Audi Hungaria's lean production system is actually so well regarded that it formed the basis for the world-wide implementation of the Audi Production System in 1999.

Production line workers at Audi Hungaria are responsible for both developing their own procedures and organizing their own workplaces, in partnership with the process engineers. This is in keeping with the empowerment philosophy that all workers in the plant make their own decisions and continually improve on their own processes (Audi Hungaria has only two reporting levels in its hierarchy).

The management's philosophy is that, within the plant, everyone is both a supplier and a customer. This means that a customer does not accept defective parts, so high assembly quality is maintained. But it also means that a customer evaluates the performance of his supplier. Therefore the logistics company which is responsible for the supply of all of the subassembly parts and components around the plant is audited every quarter by the departments that are directly affected.

Hungary for the TT

Györ, a town 130km (81 miles) west of Budapest, has become the capital of the auto industry in the country. The TT proved that it was more than capable of building a quality product. Soon the TT assembly line there was in operation six days a week, to cope with the high level of demand as Audi aimed to reduce TT delivery times to six months. The assembly of the first TT coupé began in April 1998 and there were soon celebrations of the production of the 100,000th in 2000. Over 13,000 coupé models were assembled in Györ in the first year. The third quarter of 1999 saw the addition of the Roadster. That led direct to the decision early in 2001 to manufacture high specification Audi A3 models in Hungary. With a yearly production target set for 15,000 quattros and 40,000 other models, the Györ factory has outgrown its domestic rivals and expanded into one of the most developed car assembly facilities in the region.

Audi Motor Hungária Kft, now Hungary's biggest exporter of automobiles, started manufacturing the A3 models in the middle of April 2001. Györ's annual capacity was set to go up to 55,000 cars, around 40,000 of which will be TT coupés and Roadsters, and the remaining 15,000 will be A3 models. The number of employees there has grown since A3 production was launched and soon totalled almost 5,000. Eleven hundred workers are dedicated to the production of the TT as total sales topped 140,000 in 2001. Audi's $70 million investment in Hungary has certainly paid off.

Fuelled, checked and ready to roll off the production line, into a protective bag and back on to a train for the return to Germany.

10   Sport

For the company with the four rings trademark, past and present, motor sport has always meant two things: a major technical challenge and a venture linking a company with its employees.

Dr Ferdinand Piech, chairman of the Audi
AG board, speaking in 1992

Dr Piech was always aware of the power of motorsport. Speaking in 1998, and by then the chairman of Volkswagen AG, he also said, 'Sport stimulates production and vice versa.' Few could disagree with that sentiment, especially given Audi's motorsport heritage.

Piech continued:

The history of Audi motor sport started 75 years ago with the *Alpensieger* which carried off countless Alpine Rally prizes, the Silver Arrows of the Auto Union continued this motor sport tradition. Then finally, in the early eighties, the quattros revolutionized rally sport . . . The superiority of the permanent four-wheel drive system in competition sport more than justified our development efforts . . . Today, we at Audi are proud to have helped smooth the way for this technology to become a part of everyday life . . . The Audi Sport quattro is the crowning glory of this development. The Sport quattro's similarity to its production cousin was essential for our policy of sport stimulating production and vice versa.

Future Past

Audi sought to reclaim its past by finding and even recreating its most famous racers. The legendary Auto Union Silver Arrows dominated the major races of the 1930s, winning thirty-two of fifty-four races up to the end of 1937. The battles fought out between the Auto Union racecars and the Mercedes single-seaters have gone down in motorsport history. Names such as Hans Stuck, Bernd Rosemeyer and Tazio Nuvolari are inseparably linked with the Silver Arrows.

Most of the Auto Union Grand Prix racecars built in Zwickau, in Saxony, went missing after the Second World War. All that remained were photographs, documents and five originals world-wide, including three twelve-cylinder Type D, a sixteen-cylinder Type C and a single sixteen-cylinder Type C hill-climb racing car. Audi AG acquired the last in Riga in 1995 and it may now be seen in Audi's own museum.

The sixteen-cylinder Type C from Riga served Crosthwaite & Gardiner, the British restoration specialists commissioned by Audi Tradition, as a model for an exact reproduction which was sent to the museum in Riga in return. In the meantime several lost Auto Union racing cars have been faithfully reproduced and are used, for example, for demonstrations at recreated historic races. Not only is the hill-climb car mentioned earlier used but also a twelve-cylinder Type D and the sixteen-cylinder Avus Type C Streamliner racing car, the last of which is particularly spectacular. The fascination of this vehicle is undiminished: in May 2000 this Streamliner tore around the banked curve of the famous

A 1938 Auto Union V12 D-Type Grand Prix car appearing at the Goodwood Festival of Speed in 1998. The profile, short overhangs and functional details are all very TT, but can the modern car ever emulate its forbear?

French circuit at Montlhéry. This was exactly 63 years after its premiere at the Avus circuit in Berlin in May 1937, when Bernd Rosemeyer took a car of this type to a speed of 380km/h (240mph) on the straight. This unique racecar now also has a place of honour in the museum.

Future Present

Audi needed a renaissance and chose sports cars, targeting one race and race series in particular. The American Le Mans Series offered a good chance to demonstrate *Vorsprung durch Technik* on the racetracks in one of the most important international markets. Indeed, Audi of America uses the successes in the ALMS for intensive marketing activity. Audi customers

attend each race, with the majority of the company's advertisements on American television based on the ALMS. As at Le Mans, the team under the direction of Reinhold Joest runs both 'works' cars from Audi Sport North America. Audi's customer team Champion Racing competes with a 2001 spec R8 in the ALMS.

The Le Mans 24-hour race has been run since 1923. In all, there are four categories at Le Mans. The Infineon Audi R8 belongs to the category of the Le Mans prototypes (LMP 900) – the top class of sports cars. On the racetrack, only the drivers may repair the cars; in the pit lane four mechanics may work at the car at the same time. In 1999 Audi started at Le Mans for the first time, immediately scoring a podium result with the R8R.

In 2000 the first triumph followed: the three Audi R8 sports cars finished first, second and third. In 2001 Audi Sport Team Joest captured a first and second victory in torrential rain. In 2002 Audi secured a superb first, second and third in front of 220,000 spectators. Audi became only the fifth manufacturer to win the toughest car race in the world with the same team, three times in a row – and the first to achieve this hat trick in nearly twenty years. The Audi works drivers Frank Biela, Tom Kristensen and Emanuele Pirro also wrote motorsport history: they are the first-ever driver squad to have won Le Mans three times in a row.

'Audi is proud to be the first manufacturer in the history of the Le Mans 24-hour race to call the Le Mans trophy its own', declared Dr Martin Winterkorn, the chairman of the board at Audi AG, who received the trophy from the president of the Automobile Club de l'Ouest (ACO), Michel Cosson.

At the beginning of the 1990s the ACO created the trophy presented each year to the Le Mans winner and handed back before the start of the next race. At the same time, the organizer decided that, if a manufacturer won the 24 hours race with the same team three times in a row, he could keep the trophy forever.

The 24-hour race is the highlight of the season. But the American Series, founded in 1999 by the American businessman Don Panoz, offers fans the chance to experience

A return to motorsport glory as Audi record a famous hat trick at Le Mans in June 2000, following that up with a first and second in 2001 and a first, second and third in 2002. Audi are back.

Success in the American Le Mans Series too, winning the team title in 2000, 2001 and 2002. Here is the 2002 Audi R8, driven by the ex-Formula 1 star Johnny Herbert.

the Le Mans sports cars ten further times in a year. The technical regulations that apply to Le Mans apply also to the ALMS races. Similarly, there there are also four categories, which are separately classified. At the pinnacle, however, are the Le Mans prototypes such as the Infineon Audi R8. Each car must have a minimum of two drivers. Points are awarded for the first fifteen of each class, extra points are awarded for the endurance races at Sebring and Road Atlanta. The ALMS has become one of the most popular racing series in North America and Audi took the drivers', manufacturers' and teams' titles in 2000 and 2001.

ALMS Commemorative Edition TT

To celebrate its triumphs and successes in the American Le Mans Series, Audi introduced an ALMS Commemorative Limited Edition TT in 2002. The company offered 1,000 uniquely styled 2002 TT coupés featuring special 18in wheels, high performance tyres, colour and trim. The colour and trim specification was unique with a Misano Red pearl effect exterior with a silver Silk Nappa leather interior, or an Avus Silver pearl effect exterior with a Brilliant Red interior. Other interior changes include knee bolsters, gear knob and steering wheel all in a corresponding leather.

> The ALMS Commemorative Edition TT is likely to be coveted by enthusiasts and collectors [said Len Hunt, vice-president, Audi of America]. We crafted this special vehicle to showcase Audi's successful motorsport endeavors in North America. The ALMS Commemorative Edition TT goes far beyond just design, it is a constant reflection of the exhilarating experience witnessed on the track for the past two years when Audi convincingly clinched the drivers' and manufacturers' titles in the American Le Mans Series.
>
> We are very honored that Audi has introduced the ALMS Commemorative Edition TT [said Scott Atherton, president and COE, Panoz Motor Sports Group]. Audi has been a strong marketing partner and supporter for the past two years and this latest step is a perfect example of Audi's ongoing commitment to the series.

Is that is what the TT had come to? Nothing more than a special edition, part of Audi's marketing plan, but not the racing programme. How could a car with a name so closely associated with motorsport not be in the thick of the track action. Fortunately there was a racing series and a legendary tuning company that could save the TT from motorsport oblivion.

DTM II

In the late 1990s the German DTM racing series, Deutsche Tourenwagen Meisterschaft, had lost its way. It had become prohibitively expensive to build competitive cars, which had become far too complex. The racing became predictable and the fans could no longer identify with the teams or the cars. So a new DTM series was created for the 2000 season and renamed Deutsche Tourenwagen Masters. The idea was to get back to the sport's roots.

The cars had to conform to the following specifications: they had to be two-door, mass-production models with four seats, from 4,300 to 4,700mm (169–185in) in length and a minimum weight of 1,050kg (2,265lb). The engines are 4.0ltr V8s with a minimum weight of 150kg (280lb), which will produce around 450bhp at 8,000rpm with air restrictor and driving the rear wheels through a standard six-

At Abt, they always wanted to be at the front, leaving the Mercedes CLKs in their wake, although it took a couple of seasons to get the TTs just right.

speed gearbox. The tyres are, like the gearbox, 'controlled', standard to all teams. These Dunlops have a maximum diameter of 650mm and a front width of 10in while the rears are 12in.

Abt Go TT

After winning the German Super Touring Championship (STW) in 1999, Abt Sportsline, the world's largest VW and Audi tuning company, decided that it could turn the TT into a race winner. However, it had to get special permission to use the TT because it is a rather short.

> We are convinced that the new DTM will be a great success. Therefore, we, as a team, wanted to be part of it right from the very start [explained the team boss Hans-Jürgen Abt in 2000]. I'm delighted that we got the green light from the Deutsche Motor Sport Bund following the recommendations of the Touring Car Association (ITR) and the DTM Commission. Together with Mercedes and Opel we can contribute to building up the new DTM series.

At the Abt Sportsline base in Kempten, the pressure was now on to develop the Abt-Audi TT in time for the DTM. Because approval for the project came very late, testing could begin only at the end of April, leaving less than four weeks before the first race at Hockenheim.

> The 2000 season will be a year of learning for us [Abt emphasized]. It is a huge challenge for Abt Sportsline to develop such a vehicle under our own direction. That's why one shouldn't expect miracles in the first year. In the next months we face a massive workload. But I'm convinced that Abt Sportsline has the technical competence to design and build a competitive DTM car.

That opinion was shared by his brother Christian Abt, who drove one of the three Abt-Audi TTs in the yellow corporate colours of Hasseröder:

> 2000 is a year of development for us. We want to learn as much as possible, and our aim is to be amongst the front-runners by 2001 at the latest. I'm absolutely thrilled that I can compete in such a popular racing series. That is a dream come true for me. For many years it was my greatest goal to contest the DTM. And to do this with an Audi is the icing on the cake.

B★W TT

There were rumours that Abt would revive the old DTM V8. However, the old Audi V8 had failed because its cylinders were positioned too closely together. That meant that it had to look around for alternative blocks. A tuner named Marder had developed a 4ltr V8 for BMW to use in sport prototype racing. So Abt decided to use that, but with its own components, which included the crankshaft, pistons, piston rods and cylinder heads.

While the chassis was made at a company called Fosstech at York in Britain, the engine and aerodynamics were taken care of at Abt Sportline team's base in Kempten in Bavaria.

The drivers for that first season were the reigning STW champion Christian Abt, the ex-STW champion Laurent Aiello, Christian's STW teammate Kris Nissen, and James Thompson drove the fourth TT from the Nurburgring event on. However, 2000 provided a steep learning curve, with very average performances and few points scored, but at least the team got plenty of valuable experience. Things would have to change in the next season.

2001 'Touring Car of the Year'

There were several changes in their second year of competition as the team were allowed to use a huge rear wing and a longer wheelbase by 17cm (6.7in). The Abt Team now consisted of two 'old' drivers, Christian Abt and Laurent Aiello, who were joined by Mattias Ekström and Martin Tomczyk. Over the 2001 DTM season the Team Abt Sportsline secured a total of two victories, five podium finishes, and started three times from pole position. Three Abt drivers finished the season in the top ten of the championship, with Laurent Aiello holding the runner-up position and with a real chance of the title right up until the final round. And another record: at five race weekends Abt Sportsline managed the fastest pitstop, and with a time of 5.588sec set the 2001 record.

Just weeks after the season final of the DTM the Abt-Audi TT-R again hit the head-lines: Readers of the on-line magazine racing1.de chose the 450hp DTM racer of the Abt Sportsline team as the 'Touring Car of the Year 2001'. Securing a sensational 36 per cent of the votes, the TT-R relegated the Mercedes CLK DTM to second place. The car of the previous and newly crowned DTM champion Bernd Schneider received 26 per cent, from a total of vote of 4,500.

'I'm particularly delighted about this award because it comes directly from the motorsport fans', Hans-Jürgen Abt declared. 'I would like to thank the spectators for their choice and their support over the entire season.' Abt immediately followed up with a promise, 'This year we beat Mercedes with the readers' choice – next year we want to beat them on the track.'

2002 DTM

After just two years the new DTM series was winning over spectators, as some 540,000 turned up at the race tracks in the 2001 season, and it was a television success as around 1.3 million watched each race. Abt Sportsline was very confident: 'When you win races the next step is the championship,' Abt

said. An ambitious goal, particularly when faced with the fierce competition in Germany's top touring car series. Abt added: 'I'm absolutely certain that we are heading into the toughest year of the DTM. Mercedes is, as before, the yardstick. Opel will again be up the front and has several things up its sleeve. We will have to give everything we've got from the first race on if we want to be among the front-runners.'

The motorsport department had almost doubled in size in order to provide sufficient space and working conditions to assemble five new Abt-Audi TT-R cars. Partnering them was the renowned British engine builder Neil Brown, of Spalding, Lincolnshire. Another British company, Hewland Engineering, of Waltham, Berkshire, builds Audi's six-speed sequential transmission.

The engineers left the basis of the previous season's winning car untouched and limited themselves to intensive work on details. 'We won twice in 2001 and raced at the front at all rounds. That's an excellent starting position from which to further refine the vehicles', said Hans-Jürgen Abt. The drivers were the former British Touring Car Champion Laurent Aiello, ex-Grand Prix driver Karl Wendlinger, Christian Abt, Mattias Ekström and Martin Tomczyk.

Champions 2002

Abt Sportsline were crowned DTM-champions for the 2002 season after their success at Zandvoort. The victory of his teammate Mattias Ekström allowed Laurent Aiello to secure the title with one race to go. With a dominant fastest time in qualifying, Aiello laid the basis for his early title win. However, the situation changed dramatically overnight – because the fuel sample taken on Saturday evening was not identical with the specification allowed for Zandvoort, the points leader was banned from participation in the

The Abt Audi TT-R up close.

qualification race and could start the main race only from last place on the grid. The apparent reason was left-over fuel from the testing that had mixed with the racing fuel. Although overtaking is known to be extremely difficult, Aiello made up from twenty-first to sixth place and even scored one point with this inspiring performance.

Perfect teamwork finally made Aiello the new DTM champion. Christian Abt and Mattias Ekström, who finished second and third in the qualification race and set the pace in the opening stages of the main race, played a decisive role in the outcome. While Abt, who was initially leading, dropped out of the points-scoring positions because of problems during the pit stop, Ekström had a

perfect stop performed by his crew during the mandatory tyre change, allowing him to get back on the track with a comforting margin over his main rivals. After an error-free drive, the 24-year old Swede celebrated his maiden DTM victory, thus achieving his self-set goal for the season and helping his team mate Aiello to secure the title early, who later said:

> Today, all my thanks go to my teammates, who helped me win the title. It was really hard having to watch during the qualification race. It was all the better to see how Christian and Mattias were fighting for me. I am proud to be a member of the Abt family and to be able to celebrate the championship with this team.

114

Abt–Audi TT-R Specification 2002

Bodywork:	tubular space frame with integrated CFC driver safety cell, integrated safety concept with crash boxes front and rear	**Weight:**	1,080kg (2,387lb) including driver
Suspension:	double wishbone axle front and rear, central wheel mounting, adjustable anti-roll bars front and rear, dampers with adjustable compression and rebound, power steering	**Wheels:**	BBS, front 9in × 18in, rear 11in × 18in
		Tyres:	front 240/650 R18, rear 280/650 R18
		Length/width/ height:	4,322/1,850/1,201mm (170.2/72.8/47.3in)
		Wheelbase:	2,600mm (102.4in)
Brakes:	front internally-vented carbon discs (380mm [15in]), rear internally-vented carbon discs (340mm [13.4in]); six-piston aluminium brake, callipers front; four-piston aluminium brake callipers rear (manufactured by AP)	**Track:**	1,615mm (63.6in) front; 1,539mm (60.6in) rear
		Tank capacity:	70ltr (18.5 US gal)
		Engine/ cylinder:	Abt V8 DTM engine, front longitudinal, 90 degree cylinder angle, cylinder spacing 102mm (4in), four OHC, time chain
		Valves:	4 per cylinder
Aerodynamics:	aerodynamic modifications to the front spoiler and side flares, flat underbody, rear diffusor, DTM standard rear wing, Abt TT-limited rear spoiler	**Displacement:**	3,998cc
		Bore and stroke:	93mm × 73.6mm
		Compression:	13.6:1
		Power output:	*ca.* 455bhp (335kW) at 6,800rpm
		Air intake restrictor:	2 × 28mm diameter
Transmission:	rear-wheel drive, longitudinal transaxle six-speed racing gearbox (manufactured by Hewland), straight-toothed, unsynchronized, sequential gearshift pattern, gearbox ratios fixed, variable final drive ratio; carbon-fibre clutch; mechanical locking differential	**Maximum torque:**	*ca.* 375lb ft at 6,000rpm
		ECU:	Bosch MS 2.9.2 (DTM standard)
		Emission control:	Lambda probe three-way catalytic converter
		Lubrication:	dry sump
		Performance:	0–60mph in 3sec; top speed 256km/hr (160mph)

11 TTLC – Tender Loving Care

The TT is by far the prettiest car we have had at the racing school and that means that the students not only want one, they also seem to treat them with a lot more respect.

Johnny Mowlem, racing driver and instructor

If you are a TT owner, then lucky you. If you plan to own one in the near future then you have a lot to look forward to. Whether you know it all or are completely clueless, here are some suggestions for making the quality of life better for a TT. After talking to the experts we have discovered just how a TT will go quicker, can be kept cleaner, can be driven more safely and bought used without worry. Here is our guide to giving any TT some real tender loving care.

TT Care: Paintwork

Your TT has a beautiful body, keep it that way. Anything you do that can wash away the road grime, salt and residues that build up on the body will help you to prolong the paint finish and your TT's useful life. Washing your TT regularly not only removes the dirt you can see, but oxidation takes effect as the sun's UV radiation falling on unprotected paintwork causes it to fade and become thin. Ideally, to park your TT in a garage or under a cover is the best defence. However, a regular maintenance regime that involves washing, polishing and then protecting the paintwork with a barrier coat of either a wax or polymer sealant is the only way to keep your TT pristine. Doing this every two to four months maintains the barrier to repel those contaminants and reduce oxidation.

1. First tackle the tyres and wheels. Use a spray-on wheel cleaner before starting to loosen the brake dust and road grime, and then spray away. Give the TT one final hose down.

2. Get a large bucket, add the shampoo and fill the bucket with lukewarm water; water that is either too hot or cold can damage the finish with hairline cracks. Never use washing-up liquid. There are plenty of shampoos on the market specifically for car washing and you probably have a brand that you are happy to use (Audi has its own range of car-care products) and follow the instructions.

3. Ideally park your TT in the shade and on an incline. This prevents water spotting and streaking as the water runs away more easily.

4. Wet the TT with a little water. Then wet a sponge with the shampoo water. Start at the top, cleaning the roof, windows and boot first. Then, before the suds dry, spray them with the hose. Continue with each side, from front to back, and then finish up with the bonnet last to avoid water spots.

5. Finally dry the car to avoid those water spots; use either a clean towel, chamois or synthetic chamois.

It should look like this.

6. If you need to remove tar from paintwork try margarine over the tar marks, leave for a couple of hours and then wipe off with a damp cloth.

TT Care: Wax

1. Once your car is clean, you are ready to begin polishing it, but first ensure that the surface is cool and dry.

2. Apply wax with a pad or cloth, preferably moistened to allow the polish to flow more easily.

3. Start with random circles and apply medium to firm pressure. Avoid getting any on rubber, vinyl or trim which may be difficult to get off.

4. Always follow the instructions on the product, but usually once the entire TT has been polished let it dry. Use two or three cleaning towels to polish off the wax. The paint could be marked by tiny scratches by buffing it with a towel that has already been used for a large area of the car through the hard, hazed wax trapped in the towel, so shake it regularly.

Keep it nice and clean like this. It makes sense.

TT Care: Interior

1.   Vacuum clean it regularly. Removing dirt, salt, dust and gravel from the carpets makes a difference to their appearance.

2.   Avoid products that make the dashboard too shiny.

3.   For cloth upholstery, steam cleaning is the answer, but it is not really practicable to do much besides vacuum clean it.

4.   With leather seats, after vacuum cleaning them, you should first clean them with a cleaner specific for the material, which contains no harmful chemicals to dull or harden it. After cleaning the leather, you should always follow up by conditioning it. Use a soft, damp cloth and apply it to the seats.

Then, if hazing occurs, buff lightly with a dry, clean towel.

TT Windows

There may not be many of them in the TT, but that makes it even more important that your view out should be a clear one. So avoid streaks by using an automotive glass cleaner which leaves no marks nor haze. Avoid paper towels with designs, which may have dyes and glues. Lint-free towels are the best bet with which to apply glass cleaner, otherwise just use plain, white paper towels. The plastic fittings inside most new cars give off fumes which can cause a haze on the windows. Sponge with vinegar, rinse with water and wipe with a dry cloth.

A pristine Roadster, and so it should be; it is brand new, but you can easily keep it this way.

TT Alloy Wheels

Ideally, a coat of wax when the alloys are brand new will to help protect the wheels and make them easier to clean. The best way to take care of them without damaging their protective finish is by frequently washing them with a mild soap and water. Periodic waxing will protect the wheels' finish from the elements.

– Never use abrasive cleansers, steel wool pads or polishing compounds.
– Beware of automatic car washes, some use acid cleaners to remove dirt and grime, others use stiff brushes for cleaning wheels and tyres.

– Never allow your wheels and tyres to be steam-cleaned because it will dull the paint and the finish on the wheels.
– Never clean hot wheels; wait until they cool otherwise the soap may dry too quickly leaving spots or a film of soap on them.
– Always clean your tyres and wheels first, one at a time. If you do this, you will not expose your washed car to the over-spray as you rinse them. Concentrate on one wheel at a time so that the soap does not dry on one while you are cleaning another. Use dedicated brushes and sponges for the wheels so that you do not damage the bodywork.

119

A beautiful sight, four TTs on the Brands Hatch track and brilliantly controlled, too: so make sure you get professional instruction like these drivers.

Driving a TT

Cleaning a TT is easy, but one vital aspect of owning one that some seem not to understand is the concept of driving it safely within their limits. That is why I spent some time at the Brands Hatch racing circuit with the racing driver Johnny Mowlem. A British Porsche Cup Champion and Le Mans and American Le Mans competitor, Mowlem knows the fastest and safest way around the track. In his capacity as an instructor he has for several years been showing everyday drivers how to handle the racing school's twenty or so TTs.

What Is the First Reaction to the TT from Your Students?

The TT is by far the prettiest car we have had at the school and that means that the students not only want one, they also seem to treat them with a lot more respect when they are compared with the previous school cars we have had.

What Problems Are There when the TT Is Driven Fast?

The TT certainly has some disadvantages when driven hard. There is less understeer (the nose of the car runs wide round a corner) than one might expect and the front bites more than expected. Lift-off oversteer (lifting your foot off the accelerator, transferring the weight to the front wheels and reducing the grip at the rear) is not huge and that means it is actually enjoyable because it can be adjusted nicely on the throttle and it is actually very stable. However, when you break heavily into corners in a TT it can be quite unnerving the first time because the front goes down and the rear end starts to waggle. On a track that is not a problem because of the big run-off areas, but you may panic on the road, especially if it is wet. On the track you have the time and space to set the car up. That means, for instance, turning in on the brakes and compressing the suspension; you don't have that luxury on the road so that you need to get to know your TT.

Another worry point would be taking a humpback bridge at very high speed. I think that, in some circumstances, without the rear spoiler the TT could swap ends quite easily. Otherwise stability is not an issue, although I have never been able to compare the unmodified TT with the current generation.

What about Front-Wheel Drive TTs?

The basic balance of the car is going to be no different. Front-wheel drive is just as effective through a corner, but if the TT does get out of shape there will not be the added grip of four-wheel drive and you will have to make adjustments with the throttle.

What Factor Does Speed Play in Driving the TT Safely?

There is a speed myth: more people make mistakes by not reading the road, say when the traffic has stopped or there is a sudden fog. At the racing school we teach control because the fact is that you can no longer drive quickly on the roads and nor should you. It is all about being smooth; the simple fact is that, once you start driving aggressively, you actually get slower. I obviously switch off the ESP when doing quick demonstration laps, for the simple reason that the car will fight against me. But in everyday road situations it is a brilliant system and there is no reason for anyone to switch it off; it really will look after you.

Is There Anything Else that TT Owners Can Do?

TT owners should look after their cars as best they can, checking for damage to tyres and regularly monitoring tyre pressures; it is as simple as that.

TT Mechanical Care

Like the racing driver said, look after your TT and it will look after you. Get it serviced on time at a proper Audi dealer, or, if it is out of warranty, then by an established and respected specialist. However, a committed owner will also keep an eye and ear on his car's performance. Any strange noises or behaviour should be investigated by an expert. Owners should also monitor all the instruments and fluid levels. Lift the bonnet on a TT and there is not much to see, but you can at least check the oil and water.

TT Tyre Care

If your TT handles strangely, especially in a heavy or sluggish manner, your tyres could be underinflated. Consult the owner's manual for the correct pressures. Do not let your tyres sink to less than 105kPa (15psi) as the tyre may overheat and deflate completely. Check for leaks by placing a little saliva on the valve. If it bubbles, you have a leak. Check the tyre tread for unusual wear and any damage to the wall.

In the United States an *Audi TT Official Factory Repair Manual* is available on CD-Rom (for Windows 95/98/NT and Mac OS) and in print form (ISBN 0-8376-6758-2); details are available at www.bentleypublishers. com.

Tuning the TT

If you are going to change the way a TT performs, one of the most effective and straightforward modifications is the art of rechipping. According to the British-based tuning experts AmD in Oxfordshire, rechipping is effectively electronic rather than mechanical engine tuning. A chip is simply an electronic storage device which is located on a circuit board inside the ECU (the engine control unit) and can be modified or remapped. Doing this is a complicated job, especially as it is not simply a case of unplugging one chip and putting in another. The TT has an ECU with 16-bit, 44-pin devices, surface-mounted on the circuit board. There is also some involved software to get to grips with. Specialist companies such as AmD have their own in-house software, desoldering equipment and many years of experience, so this is not going to be a job for the amateur.

Rechipping is, of course, just part of a total TT performance programme. The German tuners Abt Sportsline have at least five kits to enhance the output of the 180bhp version of the Audi TT. Stage one delivers 142kW (193bhp), thanks to optimized electronic engine management. Step two includes a modified air-intake manifold and a four-tube, high-grade, steel tailpipe, resulting in an impressive 151kW (205bhp). An extra 30bhp is achieved by using a larger turbocharger and a tailor-made intercooler. At the top there is the power increase up to 191kW (260bhp). From the model year 2001, the power output can be increased to 154kW (210bhp). For the 225bhp version of the TT, Abt offers a power plus resulting in 184kW (250bhp) and 195kW (265bhp), 213kW (290bhp), even up to 228kW (310bhp).

The German tuner MTM knows that exhaust systems are critical to turbocharged engines. The MTM 70mm cat-back stainless steel exhaust system combines with a stage 2 ECU software upgrade to produce 265bhp. Even more extreme is a stage 3 package that consists of MTM's full stainless cat-back exhaust, MTM exhaust manifold, turbo with external wastegate, dual flow stainless downpipe, Bosch 5 bar fuel pressure regulator, Bosch performance spark plugs, K&N air filter and appropriately modified ECU.

Power is one thing but a modified TT also needs control. MTM has springs that are progressively-wound units available for the TT to ensure comfort, lowering by 30mm (1.2in) and a firm ride. Aluminium wheel spacers improve handling by increasing the track at the front or the rear. To stop a highly modified TT, Brembo's Porsche type V-Vane discs with Porsche/Audi RS2 brake calipers, pads, stainless steel brake hoses, damping shim and mounting hardware is incredibly effective. It also benefits from stainless steel brake lines.

Buying a Used TT

There are no major worries about buying pre-owned TTs. With a full service history and a clean interior/exterior with a verified mileage all you have to concern yourself with is the price that you are prepared to pay. There are some guidelines you should follow when checking a TT, or any used car. It is always wise to consider using an expert Audi engineer to carry out a final inspection and help you to make the right decision. However, you should be able to make an initial, commonsense appraisal and decide whether this is a TT you would like to buy. One thing any TT must have is the upgrade ESP kit. Not everyone either wanted or could be bothered to let his TT be repatriated to Germany for the changes to be made. Some even preferred them in their original, pure form. That represents a tiny minority of TTs, but a vehicle without that tell-tale rear lip may prove more difficult to sell in future and may even be worth less in consequence.

TT Exterior

Start at the front and look along the sides of the TT. Are any panels wobbly? Are they misaligned? Do the same from each corner of the car, front and rear. Still standing back, compare paint matches between panels. If they are different shades then once again this could be an accident-repaired car. Finally, does it sit evenly on the road? Is there a deflated tyre, or is the suspension sagging?

Get closer. Look across the coupé's roof. The panel should be even with no signs of rough paintwork. Cars that have had major smashes often need a twisted roof to be disguised. Look for signs of paint respray around window rubbers and under wheel arches. Any excess of paint gets on to these areas when the car has been quickly resprayed. Panel gaps: are they even?

Wheels and tyres: look at the tyre tread; any uneven wear suggests that the steering is not adjusted properly, the suspension is worn or perhaps the wheels have been repeatedly thumped by a driver parking carelessly. Chips and scrapes will confirm this.

TT Interior

Make sure that everything works. It sounds obvious, but it will pay to be very methodical about this. Sit in the driver's seat and press every knob and twist every switch. Try them, most people forget to, and in a TT there is no better environment within which to check everything out. We have heard about fuel gauges that malfunction and other minor electrical glitches from the heater to the fog lights, so make sure that they work.

Condition: look at the trim and upholstery. We have heard about some loose trim, especially on the doors involving the latches and also speaker fittings and connections. Does it look fresh or rather worn? What you have to do is to decide whether the car looks like it

Fiddle with everything.

has covered as many miles as the seller says it has. You may have heard of 'clocking', which is altering the recorded mileage so that the car is worth more. Even if the paperwork seems to be conclusive the interior could tell a different story, so look for unusual or excessive wear on the seats, seat belts, steering wheel and on any other trim. If you have any doubts, contact any previous owners to find out as much as possible about the TT's history.

Under the Bonnet

There are not many checks that you can make, especially as there is a huge cover over the engine. However, with the engine cold, pull out the dipstick and look at the oil. If it is black, dirty or burnt, then the car has not been serviced properly. If the level is low then the car is either using lots of oil or someone is not maintaining it very well. Now look at the oil filler cap: it should be clean. Any black 'treacle' or white sludge means that not much has been done in the way of servicing. Look at the water: if it is brown, no anti-freeze has been added and the water seldom changed. Watch out too for white deposits which suggest a problem. Look underneath the engine: are there any oil or water leaks? Start the engine: a light metallic tinkle is fine, but a worn engine will crash, bang, click and clatter. Now walk around to the exhaust and ask a friend to rev hard and then back off suddenly. Lots of blue smoke, rather than a light haze, means serious engine wear.

There is not much you can see from looking under the bonnet of a TT, but at least you can check the fluid levels.

Don't forget to drive the TT before you buy.

Drive the TT

Remember to turn the radio off so that you can hear what is happening. Make sure that you go for a proper drive, at least an hour long. You will not learn anything from a quick drive around the block. Try to experience as many different road conditions as possible, from town to motorway.

Switch on the ignition: all the warning lights should come on (oil, ignition, brakes, and so on); if not, perhaps the seller has disconnected some? Once the engine has started all the lights should go out, immediately. Otherwise the engine is very worn. Furthermore, if the engines takes an age to start, the battery, or the expensive starter motor could be on the way out. Any rough running could mean more problems to do with tuning, or perhaps a very worn engine.

Power steering? While stationary, turn the wheel from lock to lock. If there are many squeals and strange judders then the system may be very worn.

Is getting into gear a problem? Lots of noise, lots of free play in the lever and grinding all indicate a worn and well-used gearbox. With the gears in neutral, press down the clutch pedal and listen; any whirring noises also suggest serious wear. As for the clutch, put the handbrake on and engage first gear; if the car does not stall and there is a nasty smell, it may need to be replaced.

Brakes: try them as you pull away. If they sound as though they are dragging, perhaps the car has been standing for a long while and the brakes may have seized. Lightly touch the brakes: if you hear an intermittent rubbing, it suggests brake disc damage. The ABS warning light should go out very soon after the car is started. If not, there could be a problem.

Steering: if there is any juddering as you drive along, or if, when you release the grip on the wheel on a quiet, flat road, the car pulls to one side, then there could be a simple cure, such as a cheap wheel balance. Alternatively, it could mean that the car has been involved in an accident and the suspension is bent.

Suspension: drive over rough tarmac and listen for clonks and bangs, and watch out for too many bounces. All these suggest that the suspension is tired and needs an overhaul. If you can, ride in the back of the car and listen carefully for noises there too.

Acceleration: look in the rear view mirror, is there much blue smoke? If so, the engine is very worn, although white steam is normal on a cold morning. Any squeals could mean a simple slipping fan belt, or that some expensive pumps and bearings could be on their way out. Listen for a whistling turbo, which could be very worn, especially if the car takes an age to accelerate and there is smoke pouring from the rear.

If the car is clean, tidy and, according to your companion checklist, looks a reasonable prospect, then, to avoid making a serious and expensive mistake, it is time to pay for a professional engineer's inspection. He will give you a written report on the car's condition, a valuation and most will also carry out independent checks to make sure that the car has not been not stolen, is not an insurance write off, or is still subject to a finance agreement. If you are lucky enough to get yourself a TT at the end of all of that, then drive responsibly, keep it well maintained, modify sensibly and, above all, enjoy it.

12   Speciality

The TT is a unit, clear, absolute. Add something and there's too much. Subtract anything and you destroy it.

Peter Schreyer, Audi design director

Schreyer is right: the TT is just perfect the way it is. However, not everyone agrees. Even Audi has come up with its own profitable option packages. But at least there is little interference with the purity of the original design and, in any case, what they do must be acceptable, because they designed and built the TT in the first place. As for some other companies, what they do to the TT is not just questionable, it is almost objectionable too. Some of it is so far out there that it deserves a standing ovation. But let us start by looking at what Audi has been offering owners who want something more than a ground-breaking design icon.

Authentic TT

According to Audi, drivers of the TT never cease to be fascinated by its pure design and clear lines, which is certainly true, but they continue: 'The sheer uniqueness of this design veritably incites drivers to place their personal imprint on their car.' The extensive customization range comes from quattro GmbH, a wholly owned Audi subsidiary responsible for special styling, accessory and engineering projects. The range includes exclusive leather equipment for both the Coupé and the Roadster quattro, with a free choice of colour,

and authentic leather with moccasin stitching in the standard colours.

Controls, such as the steering wheel, gear lever knob and handbrake lever, as well as the knee cushions on the centre console, may be ordered with leather upholstery. The extended leather specification, which includes the underside of the instrument panel, the door trim elements and the side or rear trim panels, is, moreover, available in leather or Alcantara. The new programme allows customers to create a car with a specification that is virtually 'tailor-made'.

Accessory TT

Not only that, there is also the quattro GmbH accessories programme which, says Audi, 'adds touches of individuality with its distinctive products. And best of all it optimizes the car's utility value so that it is tailored precisely to the driver's very personal needs.' That is why they developed a rear-mounted rack of attractive matt-chromed steel tubing specifically for the TT Roadster. This rack, with its integral brake light, can be combined with a carrier for skis or snowboards, which certainly gives that 1950s sports car look.

A tonneau cover for the TT Roadster is another practical solution offered by quattro GmbH. This cover for the interior is made from the same anthracite-coloured textile used for the standard soft top. The tonneau cover can be divided so that the passenger's side may be kept covered while the car is in

'Tailor made': the 225bhp Audi TT Roadster quattro (pictured) features new Hibiscus Red paintwork, 18in split-rim alloy wheels and silver grey leather upholstery. All items are part of a wider options package being launched by Audi for Britain's TTs.

use. This convenient adjunct for protecting the interior against dust, dirt and rain can rapidly be folded up, and, when placed in its accompanying protective sleeve, occupies little space. There is also a washable tarpaulin cover in a matching design, which effectively protects the Coupé against dust and dirt when it is parked in the garage or throughout the winter months.

The company also offers several sets and care products for leather to protect the high-quality interior materials. These products, which are matched specifically to the individual leather colours, are part of the quattro GmbH range of accessories, as are agents for gently removing stains and grease.

But this is not simply a range of merely cosmetic or purely practical items here: the quattro GmbH engineers have developed an even sportier version of the TT's suspension.

While the vehicle body has been lowered by 20mm (0.8in), modified springs and shock absorbers give the TT even more dynamic driving characteristics. This is possibly the cure for those who believe that the TT's suspension still has several shortfalls. There are also nine-spoke alloy wheels or two-piece, cross-spoke alloy wheels with size 225/40 ZR18 tyres in the range.

If you go for that suspension option, then a Recaro bucket-type seat provides excellent lateral support, to appeal to the more enthusiastic driver.

Christmas TT

Audi did not waste any time entering the special edition fray when Neiman Marcus selected the TT coupé as a 'featured gift' for its 1998 Christmas book. A hundred, limited edition, sequentially numbered Model Year 2000 TT coupés were built for delivery late in spring 1999. Buyers of the Neiman Marcus limited edition TT were among the first retail customers in the United States to take delivery of their cars.

This limited edition TT coupé, built to American specifications, was finished in a unique Nimbus Grey pearl-effect exterior with a Moccasin Red nappa leather interior. Each car was to be specially equipped with 17in polished wheels, heated front seats, xenon high intensity discharge headlights, a Bose premium sound system with six-disc CD changer, a TT car cover, and Neiman Marcus badging.

S Line TT

'Uncompromising sportiness', said Audi, 'is the distinguishing feature of the Audi TT Coupé 1.8T quattro "S Line" which is available as a limited edition, probably until the end of 2001.' Note the use of the word 'probably'. As described in Chapter 7, in some markets the S Line turned out to be nothing more than the next model year arriving rather early and premium priced too. That's all sorted out now. What buyers got though was the 165kW (225bhp) coupé which could be ordered in exclusive pearl-effect colours of Avus Silver and Misano Red.

In addition to the TT Coupé's extensive standard equipment specification, S Line included a series of customized, sporty attributes supplied by the Audi subsidiary quattro GmbH. That meant that there was a sports suspension with the body lowered by 20mm. It sat on 18in, nine-spoke, cast alloy wheels with 225/40 ZR18 tyres. The standard leather seats were black, but they could be colour-customized in red or silver as an option. Buyers handled a smart aluminium gear knob, and they saw better at night because of the xenon headlights with titanium-coloured headlight trims. The other giveaway that this was an S Line was the emblem on the rear side panels between the door and the wheel arch.

This was the first model to encompass the S Line concept, as the name was destined to be used on future products with sports packages that would transform the look and performance of those Audis.

Roadster version of quattro GmbH's S Line.

Spanish TT

Spain was the first country to celebrate Audi's first Le Mans' victories in June 2000 with a 225bhp coupé in spring 2001. Each TT Mans, as they were known, was numbered from 001 to 100, although only ninety-nine were allocated for sale. Finished in Tornado Red, they included many of the features of the S Line, running on sports suspension set at 20mm below standard, and the interior specially trimmed by quattro GmbH. Both door cards and steering wheel were trimmed in Alcantara, and a Bose sound system was supplied.

French Le Mans

In autumn 2001 it seemed only appropriate that the French Audi market would want to celebrate those two consecutive victories in the 24-hours Le Mans races. That was why Audi launched a limited series of the TT Roadster 225 quattro: badged appropriately as the 'TT Mans'.

Available only in twenty numbered vehicles, the TT Mans received specific equipment from quattro GmbH. This TT Mans was therefore finished in a special grey, which corresponded to the colour of prototype R8 No.1, which was the victorious Audi of the preceding 24hr race. Also part of the package were 18in alloys, sports suspension, red leather sports seats in red, just like the cockpit of that of prototype R8. There was an electric hood as well as a hardtop, an Alcantara trimmed steering wheel and a top of the range Concert Bose sound system.

Beetle

Want more room in your TT? Want a larger glass area? Want a dashboard-mounted receptacle for a flower? Then you are the perfect candidate for the TT Beetle – or Punch Bug, as it is known to some. The creation of a Canadian company, AKA Mad Dog Inc, it is not for everyone.

The conversion comes as a bolt-on kit and in around 30hr you can convert a Volkswagen Beetle into a Beetle TT. It is simply a matter of removing the old parts, such as the mudguards, bumper skins, boot and bonnet skins, and the headlamp covers, and fitting new ones. It may take 6hr to take off the old parts and the rest to install the new ones, ready for painting. Or the parts can be repainted to match the bodywork before they are fitted. All you need to make the final transformation is to buy an Audi TT grille and tail lights from your local dealer.

Targa TT

Although no one mentioned the T-word, this was a pleasant surprise at the 2001 Frankfurt Motor Show. Magna Steyr, an Austrian company in Graz, showed this fascinating concept. Called 'Open Sky', the roof is split into two symmetrical parts and remanufactured from glass fibre so that it may be removed easily and stored in the boot.

Postert

The German tuner Postert has a wide range of upgrades for the TT. For the roadster there are new roll bars. These stainless steel items are expensively electropolished; they not only differ in their gleaming surface from the standard roll bars but they also have a larger diameter at 76mm (3in). Easily mounted on the original fixing point, these roadster bars are fully homologated by the German TÜV.

Postert's wheel and aerodynamics kits are available for all TT Coupé and Roadster models. A front spoiler with larger air intakes not only looks different, but, it is claimed, further reduces the front axle lift. At the back, too, Postert designers have developed a rear wing which generated more down force at the rear axle.

As for the light alloy wheels, the range stretches from the one-piece 7.5J×17 wheel up to a modular 9.5J×19 wheel for the rear axle. Lowering the TT by around 35mm (1.4in) with a Postert kit, shows off the wheels well and the progressive springs are precisely tuned for each model. Postert has

also developed a height-adjustable spring strut suspension for the more demanding TT owner.

For a more sporty sound and, Postert claims, 'a more exciting look', a stainless steel sports silencer with central 135mm × 75mm (5.3in × 3in) exhaust tip is available for all front-wheel-drive TTs. The sports exhaust comes with a rear cover with matching cutout.

Abt TT–Limited

If you fancied a DTM (German Touring Masters) car for the road, then there was only one firm that could help: Abt Sportsline and the car was the Abt Limited. 'Our aim with this model is to offer a car for the street with the fascinating flair of the DTM', said Hans-Jürgen Abt, general manager of Abt Sportsline.

It certainly looks the DTM part finished in Imola Yellow. It also has a yellow-lacquered front grille with two struts, a single wiper featuring a yellow spoiler, black side indicators and door handles, as well as the unmistakable Abt emblem on the front grille and a TT-Limited insignia on the rear apron. The STW champion and DTM driver Christian Abt applied his expertise in developing the height-adjustable sports suspension, which provides a lowering of up to 45mm (1.8in). Abt also manufactured an exhaust manifold with four tail pipes and rear wing exclusively for this model.

The distinctive yellow colouring dominates the interior as well. Yellow stitching enhances the ergonomically-designed steering wheel, with the seats and floor mats trimmed with yellow seams. The instrument rings and needle fixing pin sport the yellow colouring, with the yellow running boards decorated with the TT-Limited logo. Rounding off the package are the Abt A25 sports rims (8.5in × 18in) with Dunlop sports tyres SP9000 measuring 225/40R18 (front) and 255/35R18 (rear) and Abt valve caps.

Customers could order through their local Audi dealer as well as direct from Abt Sportsline. The company also offered enhanced power output for both engine versions, up 25bhp (from 180 to 205bhp), with the power output of the 225bhp version increased to 250bhp.

Abt TT Sport

For those buyers who wanted a TT that was a little more touring than road car, Abt Sportsline developed the 300bhp Abt TT Sport. Interestingly it was also available as a roadster. The 300bhp at 6,400rpm was the result of a revised electronic engine management, supported by a modified exhaust manifold, turbocharger, intercooler and injection system. Contributing to the power-plus was modified air-ducting. The maximum torque of 294lb ft was reached at 2,800rpm. There was also a four-pipe exhaust system made of stainless steel with metal catalytic converters.

Much work in the wind tunnel resulted in optimized aerodynamics, providing considerably more down force and driving stability at high speeds on motorways and other roads. A carbon fibre body kit comprised a very low front apron, a large rear wing and a diffuser under the rear – contributing to increased safety.

For the road the ride height of the Abt TT Sport was lowered by 40mm (1.6in), compared with the standard model. Sport suspension with stronger anti-roll bars, sports brakes, a safety bar made of polished aluminium and a single windscreen wiper were part of the motorsport influence. The Sport ran on ContiSportContact tyres, 235/35-19 at the front and 275/30-19 at the rear. Inside were Recaro sports seats, featuring a combination of fine Nappa and Alcantara leather. The Abt logo was engraved on the fuel cap, the gear lever knob and the shifting gate ring.

TT-R

In 1999 at the Frankfurt Motor Show, Abt showed an incredible TT-based concept badged as the TT-R. A tuned biturbo V6 in the form of a twenty-four-valve Volkswagen VR6 unit was mounted transversely, producing approximately 350bhp and 280lb ft of torque. Abt's own exhaust system was made up of double twin stainless steel pipes equipped with two metal catalysts. The transmission was a six-speed system with Tiptronic-type steering wheel shift control with digital gear indicator. Ratios were modified to suit the car's differing horsepower and torque curves. The performance was reckoned to be 0–100 km/hr (62mph) in 5sec and a maximum speed of 286km/hr (179mph).

Obviously Abt had upgraded the car's brake system to their own sports brake package. Adjustable shock absorbers were installed on the car with sport springs which lowered it by 50mm (2in). Reinforced and adjustable stabilizers were also part of the package. In touch with the ground were 19in versions of Abt's own five-spoke wheel. The front wheels, 9in wide, were shod with 235/35-19 Conti SportContacts, while the rears, 10in wide, had 275/30-19 Contis.

Abt also used the car to showcase its own TT ground effects kit, which was designed in a wind tunnel to achieve improved aerodynamics and increased down force. The kit was made of carbon fibre for minimal additional weight and increased strength. It consisted of a new front spoiler, front grille, flared fenders, side skirts, rear skirt, rear diffuser and rear wing. The only other noticeable modification was Abt's single-armed wiper set-up. Inside, the car featured custom leather/Alcantara seating, including Abt-Recaro sport seats.

There is an engine in the boot too, and it will do 340km/hr: welcome to the MTM Bimoto.

The speedometer was another Abt piece that reads up to 310km/hr (194mph).

Hofele-Design

This was another German company making a difference to TTs with its quality products: a front bumper with integrated sport grille and headlamp covers, fixing at the original Audi fixing-points by screws. Running on Hofele-Design-Edition 2, two-piece, INOX-steel ring polished alloy wheels, the company also supplied sports suspension, with adjustable heights, lowering by up to 30–50mm (1.2–2in) at the front axle and 50mm at the rear. At the back were four exhaust pipes finished in stainless steel. These were installed by welding with a newly formed rear apron. The rear wing is an interesting new shape, with aerodynamic edge.

SGI TT

SGI (Styling Garage Ingolstadt) are also at the forefront of alternative TT technology. The most obvious change is the debadged radiator grille, headlight screens and deeper front spoiler, although a smaller one may be ordered. Larger air intakes are the basis for an increased engine performance. Radically changing the air circulation, installing a K&N sport air cleaner, engine electronics and a sport exhaust system, boosted output of the 180bhp engine to 218bhp. In the all-

important 80 to 120km/hr (50–75mph) acceleration times were cut by 1.5sec. The maximum speed was 239km/hr (149mph) and getting to 96km/hr (60mph) took just 6.9sec.

Antera alloys dramatically helped the unsprung weight of the TT. The front wheels are 8in × 18in with 225/40 tyres, while at the back 9in × 18in alloys had 255 section tyres. The suspension was stiffened with extra stabilizers. The rear wing also contributed to the stability of the car since it can be electronically adjusted.

MTM Bimoto

Probably the most outrageous TT was created by MTM. The name Bimoto gave away what this TT was all about: twin engine power. With four-wheel drive, but instead of one engine driving all four wheels, each axle had its own 1.8 turbo powerplant. You cannot miss the rear engine, viewable through the tailgate, which is positioned where the rear seats and boot used to be, transversely mounted and working through an axle that is almost identical to the front one. The TT had to be reinforced with metre-long metal tubes running along the sills from the rear to the front A panel. The passenger and the driver, sitting on Recaro seats with full racing harnesses, were separated from the rear engine by a carbon fibre wall.

Each engine was tuned to produce 326bhp

MTM Bimoto Specification			
Engine		**Tyres:**	front 245/40 ZR18, rear 245/40 ZR18
Configuration:	2 × straight 4 turbo		
Displacement:	2 × 1,781cc (108.7cu in)	**Weight:**	1,495kg (3,304lb)
Power:	2 × 326bhp @ 6,450rpm	**Weight-ratio:**	2.3kg/bhp (436.1bhp/ton)
Torque:	2 × 299lb ft (2 × 404Nm) @ 3,200rpm		
Compression		**Performance**	
ratio:	8.9:1	**Top speed:**	340km/hr (212mph)
bhp/ltr:	183.0	**0–100km/hr**	
Bore/stroke:	81.0mm × 86.4mm	**(0–62mph):**	3.6sec
		0–200km/hr	
		(0–125mph):	13.9sec
Powertrain			
Layout:	front + rear engine, all-wheel drive	**General**	
		Price:	DM250,000
Gearbox:	2 × 6-speed, manual	**Units built:**	1

and together amounted to a huge 652bhp, even though the full potential was stated as being 420bhp each for the four cylinders. The maximum speed of the MTM bimoto was in excess of 340km/hr (212mph), operating through a six-speed manual transmission. Bringing it all to a halt was the brake set-up from the Audi R–S 4. Available in theory to the buying public in 2001, it would cost a substantial DM250,000.

HMS TT

Yet more fast cars from Germany, even though their slogan is 'more than just fast cars'. They created a biturbo-V6 producing an alarming 485hp. Using the 2.8 engine from the Volkswagen Golf V6 4-Motion, there was still room enough to install two KKK turbochargers. Using special connecting rod bearings and a reduced compression, the engine will not detonate. When it does explode into life though there is that incredible 485hp and a torque of 938lb ft. In performance terms that means, with the quattro drive train, it will reach 100km/hr (62mph) in 3.8sec and 200km/hr (124mph) in 13.6. The top speed is 307km/hr (192mph).

There is a Porsche GT2 front brake with a 380mm disc and more Porsche stopping power at the rear with a 322mm disc; 8.5in × 19in BBS Le Mans rims have the required space for all that breaking power and the dimensions to offer space for the enormous brake assembly and they wear sufficient rubber which is 225/35 YR19.

13　Culture

You use the same dynamic principles and pro-
portion that you would use with a car [that] you
would use with a shoe.

Derek Jenkins, assistant chief,
Audi Design Studio, California

Never before has a car so quickly become part of the cultural landscape. The Mini took a few years to become genuinely acceptable, and only the Jaguar E-type managed to have the same immediate impact, going from a Geneva Motor Show star to an international style icon overnight. Not surprisingly, the media and artists picked up on what the TT was all about straightaway. Soon the TT became the star of advertisements, campaigns and major films. Indeed, the TT has been turning up in the most unexpected places. Within the space of a few days of watching television I spotted the TT in several programmes where it was crucial to the plot. First I saw a TT Roadster in the darkly comic *League of Gentleman* series, where it was a metaphor for cosmopolitan success. Next the Audi turned up in the equally dark, but not so funny American sci-fi series *Dark Angel*, where a TT coupé looked like the shape of personal transportation to come. The prime factor for Audi regarding the TT was to change the way consumers thought about the company and its products. Having carried out studies as to who was buying it, research in the most important market, the USA, revealed that the average age of the buyer was 40, his average income was $100,000 per annum, 70 per cent were educated to degree level, 70 per cent were men, 60 per cent married, and, given the two-door, tight fit nature of the coupé, only 20 per cent had children.

BauHouse

With that sort of profile, it is no surprise that when the Design Museum in London launched its major exhibition in 1999, a Bauhaus retrospective, Audi was the sponsor. Not only that, it used the exhibition to launch the TT Roadster in Britain. The high-performance sports car has a retro look and styling but, according to Audi, the influence of the Bauhaus movement, which aimed to combine design and function, runs much deeper.

Peter Schreyer, director of design at Audi, said: 'It is impossible to underestimate the contribution the Bauhaus School has made to modern design, and, as such, any modern designer could indeed claim a Bauhaus influence. At Audi, however, the marriage of form and function has been at the core of our design philosophy over the past century.' Clearly this was a case of art and business coming together. According to the Design Museum, the Bauhaus exhibition was planned well before the search for a suitable sponsor started. However, when looking for sponsors the Museum specifically scouted for companies which embodied the Bauhaus principles of form and design.

Paul Thompson, director of the Museum, was quoted at the time with the observation:

'There does not seem to be any motor manufacturer other than Audi which genuinely espouses the anti-historicist, modernist, functional ideals of Gropius and the Bauhaus at a time when so many car manufacturers are resorting to pastiche and retro styling.'

Awards

That may explain why the TT immediately began to pick up awards. At the Product Design Awards 1999, the iF Industry Forum Design Hanover awarded the Audi TT coupé the iF Seal of Approval for design excellence. The iF Industry Forum Design Hanover, which was set up in 1953 under the name *Good Industrial Design*, is regarded throughout the world as one of the leading bodies in the field of industrial design. Each year, with its Product Design Awards, the iF bestows its approval on products of outstandingly functional and innovative design. An international jury, including the designer Paloma Picasso, assessed a total of 1,364 products from twenty-eight countries. Of these, 224 received the coveted iF Seal of Approval.

The award was presented at the CeBIT exhibition in Hanover during a celebration event involving around 300 guests from the worlds of industry, politics and design. It was Peter Schreyer who commented:

> We're delighted by this award. It confirms yet again Audi's high standard of design. For us, the Audi TT Coupé is the realization of a vision. We've developed it without compromise, with passionate commitment and a love of detail, all the way from the design study to the production model and we've created a modern sports car that will arouse fascination and pure emotion.

Audi was no stranger to winning the prestigious iF award for design excellence, which was conferred on both the Audi A3 and the A6.

Then *Popular Science* magazine presented Audi with a 'Best of What's New' award for 1999. Audi of America, Inc. received this award for the technical prowess and innovation represented by its new TT coupé. The TT was among a hundred winners out of the thousands of entries received by the editors of the periodical in that year across a wide range of product categories.

The then new TT was described as 'Pure, Unabashed, Authentic, Attainable'. This Best of What's New award added to the TT's already impressive list of achievements. Since its introduction, the TT has been recognized for a number of awards, including a *Consumer's Digest*'s 'Best Buy' award, one of *I.D.* magazine's prestigious design awards, and was even recognized by *Metropolitan Home* magazine for its outstanding design.

The Design Centre of North Rhine-Westphalia voted the Audi Design Team its '1999 Design Team of the Year'. Schreyer received the award on behalf of the design team. 'Audi Design has succeeded in developing a distinctive, clearly identifiable formal idiom', stated the Centre as the reason for its decision. It commended Audi's success in transforming its image in recent years by overtly placing emphasis on design, and perceived this as evidence that Audi had acknowledged how design played a major part in its success, over and above being merely a matter of outward appearance.

Only two cars have ever been honoured by British Design and Art Direction (D&AD) in its history, both were Audis and the first was the TT coupé, followed a year later by the A2. D&AD is a professional association and

opposite *Audi was always keen to stress the modern architectural element of the TT's design, but critics also pointed out that form and function were not much in evidence, because this was just another cramped sports car that was difficult to see from.*

educational charity dedicated to promoting excellence in advertising and design, and to this end it rewards work which it believes 'benchmarks the very best in creativity world-wide'.

And, finally, the TT coupé quattro was voted Auto 1 in Europe for 1999. Not just because it was an attractive design and looked good parked outside a fashionable restaurant. The criteria were much wider than that. The judging panel, made up of engineers, motoring journalists, Formula One racing drivers and readers of the twelve magazines, marked the year's eligible cars on everything from driving dynamics to environmental impact and ease of repair. Their eventual shortlist included the Ford Focus, the Alfa Romeo 166 and the Mercedes S-Class; but when the final scores from all the parties were totalled it was the TT coupé quattro which secured a decisive victory.

Significantly the TT coupé dethroned Porsche as *Auto Motor und Sport*'s 'Best Sports Car of 1999' after a variety of Porsche models had held the title for twenty-three consecutive years. Some 120,000 readers chose the best cars in no fewer than twenty categories. The votes went to the TT coupé with 28.1 per cent of the readers voting for it, followed by the Porsche 911 Carrera with 26.9 and the Mercedes CLK third with only 6.1 per cent.

And obviously the TT had to pick up 'The Car Interior' of 2000 from *Auto Interiors* magazine in the USA. Worldwide, the TT has picked up many awards, although not everyone sees it as perfect.

Critics

Although the TT received plenty of plaudits, some people thought that they saw through the whole concept. Artistically interestingly, but on practical levels less than useful.

Inside it may have been fantastically detailed, but the view out of it was very com-

promised. It was pointed out that the designer Freeman Thomas was also responsible for the new Beetle which looked equally trendy on the outside, but placed the occupants in the middle at the expense of space and real comfort. And also it has to be said that with both models the design was executed at the expense of a lower drag coefficient (see chapter 7). Two design icons with a similar impact and contrasting problems: one with too much, the other with too little space.

Clearly, here are two cars that defy Mies Van Der Rohe's regularly misquoted 'form follows function' dictum. Audi go on about Gropius and the Bauhaus, citing their honesty, simplicity and purity. As any student of architecture will tell you, the Bauhaus school signified a return to the classical principles of Western architecture. Effectively it amounted to social engineering as the designers decided what was best for the occupiers. However, being told what decorations and adornments you for the most part could not have did not work. So it has been suggested that the Audi TT is all about style and does not recognize the real needs of the user/driver. What looks good on paper does not always translate into real life. Sports cars are all about what looks good. Practicality never gets a high priority. Perhaps Audi was wrong to invoke the Bauhaus, except when it came to a vehicle like the A2. Even though sales in some markets were not that impressive, to sell well over 100,000 TTs means that something about it must be right.

Although some designs need decades to mature into classic status, the TT managed that almost immediately. It does not matter what influenced the design, the simple truth is that the TT always was and always will be an icon.

Forum

With the TT Audi realized that there was a need to publicize its increasingly brave and

The striking use of the fuel filler cap as a ceiling light,
possibly on display at a Forum in your capital city.

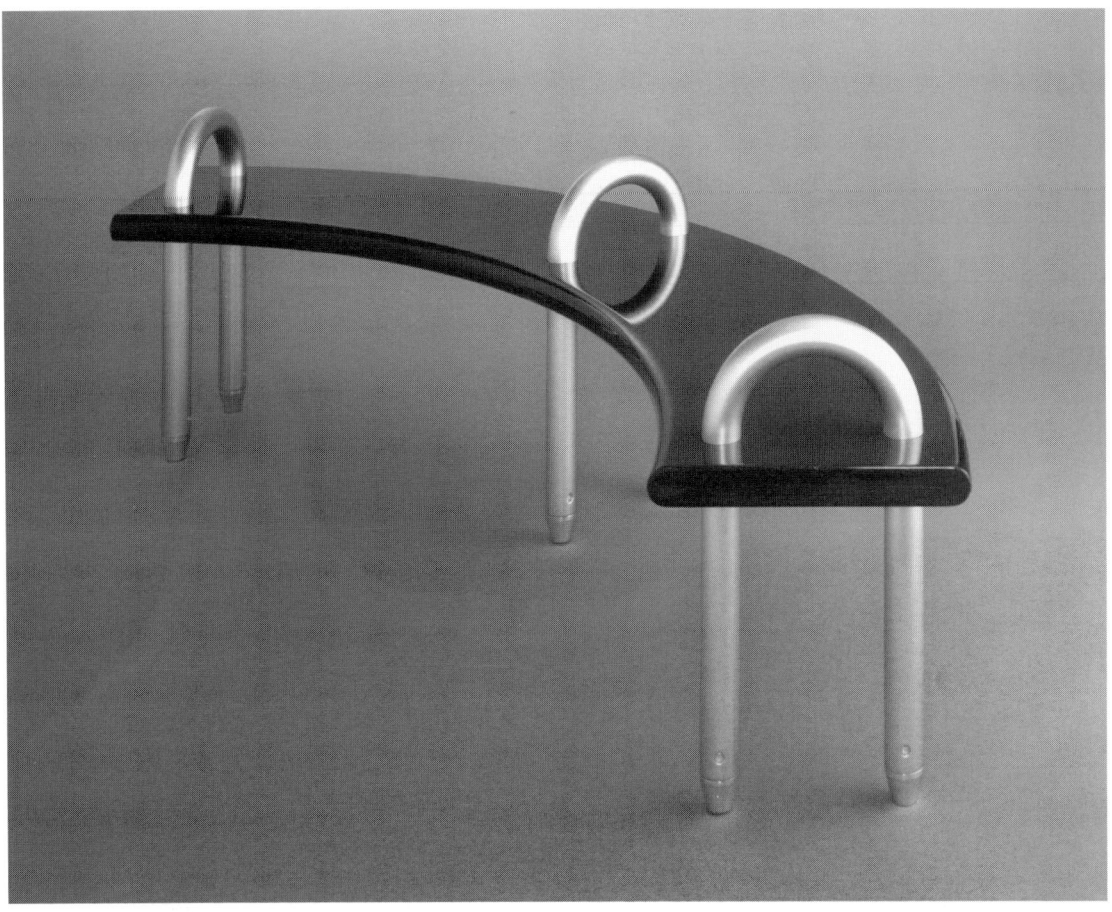

*Putting Roadster roll bars to good use, Jam Design think
laterally and practically to create this table.*

cutting edge designs and created showpiece sites around the world. The first Audi Forum was opened in New York in 1997, with others following in Paris, Stockholm, Berlin, Munich and London. The inauguration of the Audi Forum at the company's headquarters in Ingolstadt − a facility covering 77,000sq m (19 acres) at the end of 2000 enabled the Audi brand to present itself in a new light to customers, visitors and employees.

Opened in February 2002 a 700sq m (840sq yd), two-storey venue celebrating the Audi marque and all that it represented was officially opened in London. Located opposite the famous Ritz Hotel in Piccadilly, it set a new benchmark for design and decor, which will eventually be followed by the other Forum venues. As its name suggests, the new Audi Forum London will serve as a high-profile meeting place for everyone with an interest in Audi, whether on a business or a recreational basis. It will also double as a gallery and exhibition space, displaying examples of progressive design from around the world.

According, somewhat effusively, to Audi, the London Forum is the embodiment of the brand values which have, through milestone cars such as the TT quattro, positioned Audi at the forefront of contemporary automotive design. In conveying these values the aim has been to involve, inform and inspire visitors, leaving them feeling more familiar and more closely connected, with Audi.

TT Art

The London Forum has been divided into five separate areas, starting at street level with an Internet café, a boutique offering a wide range of Audi merchandise and the exhibitions and events facility. During the launch phase, part of this area was devoted to a special preview of a collection called the 'Audi Uncovered Design Initiative'. This included some specially commissioned contemporary furniture and lighting inspired by the TT Roadster quattro's famous roll bars and lights which incorporate the TT's fuel filler cap. These items came about because Audi linked with Jam Design and looked into how it could bring the Audi brand alive in a unique and memorable way. Together the two

Audi had such confidence in the TT and its marque as a brand that on this two-page magazine advertisement it relied completely on readers' recognizing the dimpled, Allen key finish.

companies co-created a brief to look into how Jam could work with existing Audi components and technologies, animating them through a range of design pieces and installations, to be used in showroom centres across Britain and ultimately further afield.

Jam was invited to undertake an exploration into the Audi brand, examining the organization, from factories and training schools in Germany, to training centres in Britain. The first phase resulted in a collection of concept ideas for both the Audi centres throughout Britain and more permanent feature designs to go into the new Audi Forum in London.

TT in Advertising

The TT has been a stunning success in advertisements, and not just ones for Audi. It has

The Audi TT: a favourite of hardcore rappers and DJs, apparently (image courtesy of Warner Brothers Music).

been used extensively in numerous other campaigns. One of the most interesting trends is how the car has been accepted 'on the street'. The TT is a 'cool' car with close associations with 'the most happening music'. That is why Warner Brothers used the distinctive shape of the coupé to adorn an album cover; *Crews Control, MC's inside the Ride*, was the title of the album and that ride turned out to be the Audi TT. A spokesman told me, 'The TT is a favourite in this scene. DJs love its street style.'

As well as promoting rap music, by contrast the TT is equally at home promoting much less confrontational products. That explains why it has been used internationally by L'Oreal cosmetics to promote their *Volum' Express* range in both television and press advertising. Agreed, that you glimpse the Roadster only briefly in the TV spot and that it forms only part of the backdrop to the advertisement, but the message is clear: beautiful people drive Audi TT Roadsters.

TT Hendrix

We have seen all the subtle and clever TT advertisements, but what about psychedelic TT TV advertisements? Third Stone from the Sun is the background to Audi's television advertising campaign, featuring Jimi Hendrix's guitar riffs and soulful vocals. This was not some cheap retro association, because from the beginning it was claimed that Hendrix, among others, was played as the designers worked. So 'designed under the influence of Jimi Hendrix' was no exaggeration.

TT Games

The TT quickly made the leap from the real to the virtual world, to become a gaming favourite. In 2000, Sony Computer Entertainment released *The Getaway* which was regarded by the experts as 'graphically impressive'. That meant that the Audi TT looked and drove like the real thing. Indeed, the TT was the only car playable on the first screenshots released to the media. *The Getaway* is a entirely hot-pursuit type game, in which the players take the role of Mark, a bank robber who is running away from his past by stealing. The graphics were regarded as far better than almost any other contemporary game.

The TT has also featured in many other computer games, including the *Gran Turismo* and *Midtown Madness* series.

TT Toys

If any car was destined to make a good looking toy then it has to be the TT. In response to popular demand, Ninco produced a slot car version of the Audi TT-R Abt, available in DTM colours. Even in Audi showrooms it is possible to buy a Rietze TT coupé plastic model car in 1:87 scale.

TT on Foot

If you need proof that the TT has influenced design, look no further than your feet, especially if they are wearing the Kobe. It started with a professional sportsman searching for the right product. That was how Kobe Bryant, NBA All-Star and member of the Lakers Championship team, came to be working with Adidas to develop a different kind of sports shoe to complement his own laid-back, confident style. Audi was then approached by Adidas in spring 1999 to collaborate on the project.

When looking for inspiration for Kobe's new shoe Adidas did not have to look any further than Kobe's roots in southern California. Adidas first asked what it was about the area that made it so distinctive? One answer was the influence of car culture. Convertibles, custom cars, surfing, there was definitely something in the Pacific air. And one of the embodiments of this lifestyle was one of the coolest cars on the market in the shape of the all new Audi TT Roadster. Remember that this was designed in part and heavily influenced by southern California. The success of the TT in that region proved that its customers could handle something new with refined style. Peter Moore, the Kobe project creative director, was quoted as saying,

The Motorsport Mini Quattro pedal car most resembles a shrunken TT.

There is no doubt, though, about what the soft toy TT is trying to be, a real softy.

Wear your TT with pride, whether it is a Coupé or Roadster pin badge, or even a TT key-ring.

Your local Audi dealer will happily sell you scale models of the real Roadster and Coupé.

Spot the TT logo on this sweater, it is hard to see the connection with our favourite car here.

'As these things [architecture and automobiles] have an influence on the other fashions within Los Angeles, those things will also begin to have more and more influence on his [Kobe's] fashion.'

Roadster Feet

Adidas certainly did something different, because instead of designing a prototype based on a marketing concept, they asked Audi to design the new shoe in the same way that they would a car. Audi's design language came into play, concentrating on simplicity and essential components such as materials, details and technologies. Derek Jenkins, assistant chief of the Audi Design Studio in California, made some interesting comments:

> I don't think people realize how complex the logistics are in designing a car. There are so many parameters to follow: whether it's crash safety or manufacturing techniques, cost or aerodynamics, they stay true to your company's identity and history. But with the shoe at the end of the day, it's really about a style. Style first, then function is as important but not as difficult to achieve.

So the two German companies concentrated on cooperating on what each knew best. 'The shoe, as a car, is a directional object', said Jenkins, 'There are only a few things in the world that are like that. It is meant to go basically in one direction. So you use the same dynamic principles and proportion that you would use with a car you would use with a shoe.' Jenkins noted that, where the lines go from thin to thick to thin to make a car look dynamic when it is moving, those same concepts were applied to the lines of the Kobe. Audi's design influence meant that, for the first time, clay models, a familiar part of the car design process, were used to prototype the Kobe.

It was soon clear that there were similarities between an Audi and this new sports shoe. Certainly the TT Roadster had three main features: a continuous line, a clean surface body side and a blunt front, to suggest the toe of the shoe. The main shoulder line continues around the arches and through the bottom of the shoe, as the Audi TT's continuous loop runs from the side of the vehicle, around the wheel arches and under the car. What Kobe had by the middle of 2000 was a new shoe: 'The sneaker is absolutely on fire . . . it's hot! It's real light and provides support for me. It's smooth, it's slick and it's different and I love it. I'm crazy for it' (Audi lifestyle articles).

Mission Possible

It did not take long for the TT to get into a major film. And Hollywood pictures do not come any bigger than *Mission Impossible 2*, starring Tom Cruise. The TT Roadster made an instant impact in the film since it was featured in a chase scene in an early part of the story, driven by Thadie Newton, playing Naya. She was up against Tom Cruise, playing Ethan Hunt, but driving a Porsche 911 Cabriolet.

The production of *Mission Impossible 2* started at the end of 1998, a time when the TT Roadster was still under wraps. Apparently four Roadsters were used and at that time they would have been preproduction prototypes. Not only that, but Audi also supplied the film production with four additional TT Roadster bodies. One Roadster was sent to Australia, then on to California, along with the other three, for the stunt scenes. Driving the TT was the stunt driver Debbie Evans, vice president of the special effects company Leavittation. This turned out to be a splendid way to show the TT to the world, as it battled on equal terms with the Porsche.

About a TT

No stunts, no stunt doubles, no special bodies were needed when it came to *About a Boy*, starring Hugh Grant. Based on Nick Hornby's bestseller, it was set in 1993, the book was published in 1998 and filmed in 2001, which caused some debate over exactly which car Grant's character Will Freeman should be driving. The book describes a 'new GTi', so there is a clue there. Grant's character is a rich, lazy philanderer who decides to target single mothers. So he invents a son, buys a car seat, sprinkles it with crumbs and installs it inside an Audi TT coupé. According to the film's producers, the character was regarded as a consummate consumer who had to have the latest gadget, but a Ferrari would not have been appropriate. Alfa Romeo Spiders and MGs were considered, as was the TT Roadster, but as some scenes called for three people in the character's car it was going to have to at least be a 2+2. The immature, if cool, character then is perfectly at home behind the wheel of an Audi TT coupé.

TT Gifts

Apparently there is an increasing demand among Audi customers for other products that are associated with their car in a looser sense. To them, the lifestyle articles that are part of the Audi collection represent a special outlook on life that goes beyond the extensive Audi model range. The Audi collection has been produced by quattro GmbH, which comprises four product lines: the Audi design collection; Audi sport collection; Audi authentic collection and Audi tradition collection.

The TT chronograph from the design collection will appeal to the individualists among watch-lovers. Its mechanical Swiss movement of calibre ETA 7750 Valjoux with automatic winder can be seen through a mineral glass base. The brushed, stainless steel case with convex sapphire glass is watertight to 5atm. A padded brown calfskin strap or, alternatively, an expanding stainless steel strap, provides an attractive finishing touch to this collector's item.

To use an overworked, ill-defined and overrated word, the conclusion has to be that the TT is 'cool'. By association, the TT gives other products credibility. On its own it is a thing of beauty and it can even involve other icons like Hendrix without bringing anyone or anything into disrepute. The TT is almost the perfect product. Easy to look at, easy to market and 100 per cent part of new millennium culture. In short, the TT is not going away. It has influenced a whole generation of new cars and new Audis.

14   The TT Effect

The Audi TT has a lot to answer for. It seems that every car-maker wants to build his own version these days. Speaking in autumn 2000, Audi's director of design Peter Schreyer said:

> For us the TT is a symbol, a precious stone . . . With its style, it has been possible to develop a formal design language, but that TT is just a small segment of the car market. That is why it has inspired the lines of the new A4 . . . The A4 needs more buyer appeal so some elements of the car's design come straight from the TT. Just take a look at the front end and the high belt line.

The A4 was hardly a TT clone, but a closer look at the 2002 Audi A4 Cabriolet certainly shows how the TT had influenced the next generation of Audis. The rear light clusters and the whole front end showed definite TT genes. Aimed at an older and more conservative market, here was a less confrontational style that was understated and undoubtedly stylish.

Schreyer also noted that many other manufacturers were paying close attention to what Audi was doing and identified the Ford Mondeo as proof that Audi was inspiring others. That only made him more determined to design products that were distinctive and thoroughly Audi, and that would explain the appearance at the Paris Motor Show in 2000 of the Steppenwolf concept.

Steppenwolf

On the face of it, the Steppenwolf would not seem to have much to do with the TT. However, this concept vehicle was meant to show how Audi's development engineers visualized a high-performance, all-rounder for the compact class. And they claimed that it embodied a study which represented the consistent evolution of Audi design. This study for the compact class also made use of Audi's quattro expertise and experience with height-adjustable air suspension. The engineers had set themselves the following goal: the Steppenwolf project should be able to master rough terrain in extreme conditions just as effortlessly as high-speed driving and it should feel equally at home in the outback as on the motorway.

A free-revving, 3.2ltr V6 engine, which would eventually find its way into the TT, developed 165kW (225bhp), just like a contemporary top of the range TT. It was supposed to accelerate the Steppenwolf from 0 to 100km/hr (0–62mph) in under 8sec and its top speed was claimed to be in excess of 230km/hr (144mph). Its peak torque of 235lb ft was available across a wide speed range. The manual six-speed gearbox turned this strength into a guarantee of excellent pulling power in every speed range.

The permanent four-wheel-drive system ensured maximum traction and excellent directional stability in all conditions and in all types of terrain. Like the TT, the vehicle

An Audi A4 Cabriolet with obvious TT Roadster influences.

embodied the electronically-controlled Haldex centre differential, distributing power between the front and the rear wheels. If the front wheels slip, part of the torque is put to the road smoothly via the rear wheels, as required.

As in the TT, there was plenty of electronic assistance, so the electronic differential lock (EDL) distributes torque between the wheels on one axle. And the electronic stability program (ESP) helped the driver to remain in control. McPherson struts and the double wishbone rear axle are similar to those on the TT, but with the addition of adjustable air suspension. Apparently the Audi engineers decided on the floor pan with a transversally installed front engine as the basis for this new model, making it the same platform as was used on the Audi A3 and TT. It is a four-seater, at 4.21m (13.8ft) long, 1.83m (6ft) wide and 1.46m (4.8ft) high, with a noticeably wider track.

The Steppenwolf is a completely new design, although the flared wheel arches are much like those on the TT. Indeed, Audi remained true to its Bauhaus convictions and claimed that,

> Anyone taking a step back will recognize the characteristics of the new Audi design in the overall form of the body: wide, clearly contoured lines and large, pure surfaces combine to produce

Those arches and that aggressive stance ... the Steppenwolf is also like the TT, a new kind of car.

an architecture in which calm and tension are equally present. No superfluous swage lines or curves upset this visual clarity. Function and form become one.

As Schreyer made clear, other car companies had been watching what Audi was doing. Since 1998 just about every magazine feature about a new, radical sports car or concept always referred to the fact that the maker was producing his own TT. In some cases it was not just a challenging design, sometimes the resemblance to a TT, whether a coupé or a roadster, was almost uncanny.

Copy Cats

The Daihatsu Copen (derived from the words compact and open) was one of the first mini-roadsters with an electrically-operated hard top. Its simple two-seater silhouette certainly shows some influence from the Audi TT, but in a more pocket-sized form. Its performance is honed through a quick-response, 660cc twin-cam, four-cylinder, turbocharged engine. The Copen is similar in size to the Cappucino, Suzuki's earlier entrant in the 'K' car segment.

The Daihatsu Copen.

Streetka

Even more of a TT Roadster shrunk in the wash was the Ford StreetKa. This is a two-door, two-seat, spider based on the Ford Ka. 'Inspiration for the StreetKa concept came from studying the diverse European youth culture and the constantly evolving trends in street fashion, music and film', said Filippo Sapino, managing director of Ghia SpA, 'We have taken the already fashionable Ford Ka and given it an urban, street spider look and feel.'

Ford called it 'New Edge' design when the Ka was first launched in 1996 because it combined smooth sculpted surfaces with clean, crisp intersections to produce a sharper, more defined image. The twin roll hoops certainly bring the TT to mind, although the inspiration was apparently the small British sports cars from the 1960s such as the MG Midget and the Austin Healey Frogeye Sprite.

Nissan 350Z

If any model were going to give the TT a run for its money then the Nissan 350Z was it. The Z cars had been legendary coupés that eventually went soft, but Nissan must have looked at the TT and decided that it could revive a great model.

Car magazine brought them together in California in the October 2002 issue. They thought that the Nissan was a good rival for the TT in terms of head-turning looks, with its neat design and proportions. 'But there's no doubt that the Z's interior does feel relatively low rent compared with the TTs . . . it's not in the same league as the hewn-from-solid Audi.'

The Ford Streetka.

The Nissan 350Z.

The TT's engine still proved responsive and had mid-range responses when compared with the smooth-revving Nissan. However, the brakes were snappier and the throttle response was still hampered by the turbo. On twisting roads, however, the TT really lagged behind:

> Take a corner in isolation and the TT can just about keep up, leaning drunkenly in the Nissan's rear view mirror. Take a sequence of corners and the Audi drops straight out of the reckoning as its driver has to defuse 15 degrees of understeer before starting on the next one.
>
> But on a straight the TT really was left in the distance.

The designer of this car was Ajay Panchal from Britain who trained at Coventry Uni-versity. Interviewed by *Car*, the designer had this to say about the 350Z: 'I think it recap-tures the idea of a sports car that look like it's moving when it's standing still.' When asked about influences he talked of stealth fighters and cutting-edge architecture. 'It's definitely not German; the whole car is about the contrast of negative shapes and positive shapes . . . I like it when things don't quite line up, I like to challenge predictability and break the rules.' But what car does *he* drive? Yes, an Audi TT; although he was soon to part-exchange it for something he prepared earlier. 'The Z is so much more than a souped-up Golf. This is the real thing.'

Chrysler Crossfire

This sleek two-seater provides the Chrysler brand with a new halo car following on from the successful PT Cruiser, and looking similar to the TT. Originally a concept vehicle shown in 2001, Chrysler's history of bringing the Viper, the Prowler and the PT Cruiser to production meant that the Crossfire stood a good chance of being built if the response were positive, and it was. A speed-sensitive rear spoiler has been incorporated to deploy at 80km/hr (50mph) to overcome any TT-like stability problems. Under the bonnet is expected to be the Mercedes 3.2ltr V6 pro-ducing 215bhp running through a six-speed manual or five-speed automatic. However, a high-speed AMG could be offered while many of the chassis components could be sourced from the Mercedes SLK.

The car's exterior was designed by 25-year-old Erik Stoddard, a graduate of the Cleveland Institute of Art. The car's resemblance to the Audi TT and the fact that the TT's creator Freeman Thomas is now vice-president for advance product design in the Chrysler group is, Daimler Chrysler claim, purely coincidental. But the Crossfire was pictured in desert testing with a white TT in attendance.

The Chrysler Crossfire.

From Coupé to Roadster, or vice versa in just a few seconds.

*The
SEAT
Tango.*

Lexus TT

Here is the cleverest TT clone: the Lexus SC430 is both a coupé and roadster rolled into one. Not surprisingly, it is more expensive with all its electronics, but it certainly cannot be described as prettier than the Audi. However, it was aimed at the higher value end of the roadster/coupé market, running up against the Jaguar XK and the Mercedes SL. The quality, refinement and even the performance cannot be questioned, but it is not as emotionally involving as the TT.

Tango and TT

Audi has even inspired other companies within the Volkswagen group to let their imaginations run wild, hence the SEAT Tango. Beneath the skin of the Tango, there is a sophisticated tubular structure developed by teams at the SEAT Technical Centre and SEAT Sport – in effect, it is an evolution of the World Rally Car safety cage. Within this structure nestles an 180bhp 1.8 turbocharged engine with a six-speed gearbox. SEAT claim the Tango has a top speed of 230km/hr (145mph) and sprints from 0 to 96km/hr (0 to 60mph) in about 7sec.

High levels of safety have been central to the development of the Tango: it features the latest generation ABS, electronic stability control, traction control, twin front airbags, side airbags, seat-belt pre-tensioners, a progressive deformation structure and a central passenger cell which is highly resistant to front, side and rear impacts.

Originally there were no plans to produce the Tango and it could have remained a concept. However, the VW management gave it the green light in late 2002, as both a coupé and a roadster. Indeed, the Tango is slated to be the sister car to the next generation TT. Under the skin, both the TT and the Tango will be a lightweight aluminium spaceframe chassis. It will be manufactured by Audi at Neckarsulm alongside the A8, the A2 and the forthcoming Supercar chassis (*see* below).

According to insiders, the new, longer wheelbase chassis offers more head and legroom and in coupé form a hatchback with four seats. The roadster will get a 2+2 layout and a folding fabric roof with a glass window. The styling of both cars will be overseen by the SEAT design head Walter de Silva, but the designs will be distinct: distinctly TT and distinctly Tango. Effectively, the Tango will be a cut-price TT without the V6 engines.

TT Supercar

Audi confirmed that it was working on an all-new sportscar that would slot above the TT in its line-up. Industry rumours suggested that the new two-door would be a reskinned version of Lamborghini's upcoming coupé, codenamed L714. The styling would be derived from Audi's Rosemeyer concept car, first shown in Frankfurt, but some of the concept's more outlandish features would be toned down to reflect a more corporate look.

Visitors to Audi's pavilion at the new 'Autostadt' ('car city') in Wolfsburg get a sneak preview, but it turns out to be the Rosemeyer car. The massive radiator grille is reminiscent of the historic Auto Union Silver Arrow racing cars. Similarly, the long engine cover falling away to the rear, with its vertical air inlet slots and the gleaming matt-finished body with its brushed aluminium surface, also conjure up images of the historic Silver Arrow cars. Not only that, it also conjures up images of a TT that has been put under a magnifying glass; the wheel arches, trademark seven-spoke alloys and shape of the headlamps are all TT-inspired.

There is certainly room under the bodywork for a rumoured W16 engine linked up to the quattro four-wheel-drive system and it

The TT Supercar.

certainly would be Audi's answer to the Mercedes SLR and the McLaren F1. The 623bhp 8.0ltr engine, which is two 4.0ltr V8s joined together, gives huge power and refinement.

The styling is the work of the design director Peter Schreyer and his team, and combines the best elements of Audi's classic and contemporary looks. Schreyer said:

> We must look very carefully at the way we approach the flagship sports car market. It must be a machine that takes Audi forward rather than backwards. Given our brand values, we don't want to build something like BMW's Z8, which in some ways takes its maker a step back.

Schreyer was right, with the TT Audi may

have glanced back, but the TT is an example of the company's moving relentlessly forward. That is why so many other manufacturers are determined to produce a so-called 'halo' product of their own. An exciting model that showcases their technology, design excellence and makes the entire marque look good. The TT is proof that well-received concept cars do not have to be parked in a garage or a museum gathering dust. The principle now is that if the show car looks good enough to build, then it probably should be put into production if budgets allow. The TT is not just the model that made Audi sexy, it is the model that has shaken up the sports car and design industry world-wide. Thanks to the TT you will not have to buy a boring sports car ever again.

Index